Mary B. Freeman

GOOGLE CLASSROOM AND ZOOM FOR BEGINNERS

An Easy Professional Step-By-Step Guide to Manage Distance Learning and Improve Your Online Lessons

2 Books in 1:

Google Classroom and Zoom for Beginners

TABLE OF CONTENTS

GOOGLE CLASSROOM (BOOK 1)

GOOGLE
CLASSROOM

AN EASY STEP-BY-STEP GUIDE FOR
TEACHERS TO TAKE YOUR CLASSROOM
DIGITAL. DISCOVER HOW TO SAVE TIME
DURING YOUR LESSONS AND INCREASE
YOUR STUDENTS ENGAGEMENTS

MARY B.
FREEMAN

GOOGLE CLASSROOM

Introduction

While distance learning could have its origins in the late 1900s, the idea of online courses initially came into operation in the middle of the 19th century when the US established a postal system. The concept of active, long-distance communications contributed to the establishment and introduction of what became termed 'private correspondence colleges,' whereby teaching missives would be circulated amongst learners and teachers via the mailing service.

Thanks to the abundance of online and emerging media, at-distance education services nowadays have become more complex and open. Prestigious colleges across the globe presently offer course materials, digital degree programs, and online courses that both legitimize and popularize the concept of computer-based schooling.

Since the late 1800s, a few significant developments have influenced and moved distance learning forward. In 1873, Ana Eliot Ticknor founded the first formal communication education service titled *Social System for Encouraging Home Studies* in Boston, Massachusetts. In 1911, Queensland University in Australia formed its communications Studies Department that depended on Australia's mail service. The University of South Africa, today regarded as one of the free online education giant-colleges worldwide, became a distance education pioneer when it reconfigured its purpose and emphasis in 1946.

In 1953, it started conducting the first broadcast college classes on KUHT (now renamed Houston PBS), which became the first public news program in the United States, the College of House made at-distance education famous. Referring to itself as "the platform that alters you," KUHT ran 13-15 hours of teaching information every week, representing about 38% of the channel's total television coverage. Most lessons broadcast throughout the evening and content was interpreted by learners who served throughout the day.

The next powerful influence to revitalize learning materials was after TV news, the desktop computer, and the private web. In 1989, Phoenix University became the first establishment to release a fully online college institution offering bachelor's and master's degrees.

In 1996, Jones International University, launched by Glen Jones and Bernand Luskin, became the next completely web-based school to be certified. Distance education has continued to expand in several different places since the development of these entirely online schools and educational institutions. The staff of the Blackboard Learning Program announced in 2003 that 40,000 teachers taught 150,000 online classes to over 6 million students in 55 countries.

The development of distance learning in university education has several essential effects. For instance, a pre-university student's profile has changed markedly. The median age of students studying at the University of Phoenix is about 33, and at the moment, more than 50% of all incoming classes are girls.

Google Classroom has a couple of Google apps that are integrated with it to make the sharing of files between instructors and their students possible. For example, an instructor/teacher can use Google Drive to create assignments as well as distribute the tasks to his/her students. Google Docs, Google Sheets, and Google Slides can be used to write. Gmail provides a platform for the files to be shared, as well as for further information to be passed across. Lastly, Google Calendar can be used to schedule the time and date where the assignments can be submitted.

Apps in mobile phones (Android and iOS) allow the students to take pictures and attach them to assignments, transfer files using other apps, and get access to some additional information offline. Teachers are also equipped to keep tabs on the progress of their students from the submitted assignments. Once they are done scoring and grading the assignments, they can return them to the students, alongside appropriate comments.

Google Classroom brings about more productivity in teaching and learning in the following ways: assignments are streamlined, increased collaboration, and advocating communication between students and teachers. Teachers or instructors can create classes, allocate assignments, send feedback to their students, and more in one place. Moreover, schools and nonprofit organizations can get Google Classroom for free since it is a core service available under G Suite for Education and G Suite for Nonprofits. It is also a service available under G Suite for Enterprise and G Suite for Business.

Tasks are stored and then graded on Google's suite of collaboration applications that enable a student to communicate with the instructor and the subject/pupil. Instead of exchanging records that exist with the instructor on the Google Drive of students, files are stored on the student's computer and uploaded for testing. Teachers should pick a file that will be used as a prototype such that each student should update their own copy and then return to a grade, instead of requiring all students to access duplicate or modify the same text. Students can also opt to bind additional documents to the assignment from their Drive. Google Classroom is essentially a free web service created for schools by Google to simplify the production, delivery, and evaluation of assignments. Google Classroom's primary purpose is to simplify the process by which teachers and students share files.

The book has been split into chapters; each chapter focuses on a particular theme, giving you a step-by-step description on handling all aspects of Google Classroom.

It explains what Google Classroom is all about and how you can benefit from what Google Classroom offers. It explains the possibilities open to Google Classroom users.

It gives a step-by-step guide on how to start up with Google Classroom. Everything is spelled out so that even if you are a total newbie, you'll get the hang of it without stress. This book explains what you will need to start a class. It also contains a summary of the major components of Google Classroom and how they contribute to the organizational flow of information.

You will be taught how to create a class. You will also be taught how to manage a class. Classes differ in size and purpose. Some classes have a few members while there are also large classes with many members. Some classes are for young learners while others are for older, advanced learners. What you will learn in this chapter and subsequent chapters will equip you to manage your classes excellently.

This book explains how to invite students and teachers to classes and how to give assignments and set due dates. Tips on how to make the class more interactive and engaging for the student are explained. An interactive class keeps the students motivated. Keeping students motivated in an online classroom is different from how it is done in a real-life classroom.

CHAPTER 1:

What is Google Classroom?

Today's technology empowers educators to step away from the conventional classroom where teachers guide and students work independently.

You may have heard of it if you're a teacher, a student, or even a parent. Most likely, several schools would turn to use this despite the current global situation.

Maybe your school is beginning to turn to that form of program. If that is the case, you will probably know Google Classroom a little bit more.

Here we'll help you to understand Google Classroom properly and how it works.

Google Classroom is a classroom software platform designed to provide a single dashboard to unify the use of other Google apps by teachers.

Google Classroom aims to encourage paperless communication between teachers and students and streamline the workflow of education.

Classroom lets teachers create classes, post assignments, organize files, and show real-time work.

One of the good features is that the Classroom is completely compatible with all other Google apps, and students and teachers can easily exchange information with each other, instead of having to jump through multiple barriers to send work. It also simplifies other features in apps. For example, using the Doctopus feature to make Google Docs will no longer need duplicate copies for students.

Google Classroom is a free resource for teachers and students to work with together. Teachers will create an online classroom, invite students to the class, then create assignments, and distribute them. Students and teachers can have discussions about the assignments inside the Google Classroom, and teachers can monitor the progress of the students. Schools must register to use the Classroom for a free account on Google Apps for Education.

Students and teachers have access to apps that aren't included in a personal Google account under Classroom software. For example, teachers can add images to questions in Forms, or as answers to multiple choices. Gmail's Inbox groups Classroom messages in the Inbox, making it easier for teachers and students to find relevant notifications and highlights. The Classroom tool also helps teachers to organize the stream of classes by adding topics to posts, and teachers and students can search the stream for different subjects.

If you still use paper to a large degree for materials and assignments, then Google Classroom provides an easy-to-use, entry-level step towards digitalizing your class. As with many of its products, Google makes every effort to have a user-friendly and self-intuitive experience. If you still use paperless approaches for your pupils, then with its peerless integration with its devices, Classroom can streamline your workflow.

The classroom is not a development tool, but rather a management tool; thus, it involves you and your students to know how to post information and records, and how to find the information you want. If your students already have experience with other Google apps, such as Docs or Spreadsheets, then Classroom is already set to use them.

Benefits of Google Classroom

Access

Google Classroom could be accessed from any computer through Google Chrome or in any device. All documents uploaded by instructors and pupils are saved in a Classroom folder on Google Drive.

Users may get any place. Students no longer need to be concerned about penalizing computers or famished puppies.

Exposure

Classroom supplies students with an exposure learning system.

Many university and college applications today require students to register in a minimum of one online course.

Exposure to Google Classroom can help students transition to learning management methods utilized in education.

Paperless

Pupils and teachers will not have excessive quantities of newspapers to shuffle because the Classroom is totally paperless.

When educators upload assignments and examinations to the Classroom, they're concurrently saved to push. Students may complete assignments and evaluations directly through the Classroom, and their job can also be saved to push. Students find and may get work because of absences.

Time Saver

The classroom is a massive time-saver. With all sources, teachers may have time to finish tasks via the capability to get the Classroom anywhere. Students and teachers may participate through their telephones or tablets, since Classroom could be obtained on a mobile device.

Communication

Tools make communication with parents and pupils a breeze. Students and teachers may send emails, post to the flow, opinions on assignments, and comments. Teachers have complete control over posts and student opinions. They're also able to communicate via emails or Classroom email summaries, including dates and course statements.

Engagement

Most natives are familiar with technology and will be more inclined to take ownership of their learning. Classroom presents methods to make learning collaborative and interactive. It provides teachers the ability to include web pages and videos into classes to differentiate assignments and make group assignments.

Differentiation

In Classroom, educators can distinguish instructions for students. When developing an assignment for groups of pupils, individual students, or the entire class, courses take only a few steps.

Feedback

Providing feedback to pupils is a component of learning. Within the Classroom's application, teachers may send feedback.

It is possible to produce a remark bank, which can be accessed inside the application. Additionally, the Classroom program lets users annotate work.

Data Analysis

To be able to make learning purposeful, teachers should derive information from assessments and understanding of learning goals.

Information from evaluations can be categorized into Sheets for analysis and sorting.

Exposure to an Online Learning Platform

Many schools require students to choose at least one class throughout the degree work. In reality, if you do a Master's degree in Education, much of your coursework might be online. Many students haven't had any experience with online instruction.

That's the reason you ought to be certain that you expose your students to it as early as possible. Google Classroom is a simple method since it's super user-friendly to assist students.

Easy Access to Materials

Google Classroom provides students access to matters that are posted online. Gone are the days of worksheets or rubrics. Absent students may easily access classroom Matters from home if needed. This really can help save you and your pupils a great deal of anxiety in the long term.

No Missing Work

Work can't be lost by pupils if they possess it. Everything is conserves as they are operating in Google Drive; therefore, excuses dwindle. Regarding how to utilize these tools, with a few lessons, students may experience success in getting organized.

Engagement

It has been demonstrated time and time again that pupils are engaged by technology. Google Classroom remains engaged in the learning procedure and will help pupils. In case you have students answer questions in Classroom, other students may comment to expand on the ideas and those replies.

Easy Workflow Management

Say goodbye to assessing or collecting assignments off a record. Together with Google Classroom, you will have the ability to keep track of assignments coming in with a glance. This makes it effortless to understand the status of everyone and also to follow up. Work is time-stamped, so overdue work can be identified.

See Real-Time Progress

Google Classroom makes it effortless to test pupils. In the Student Function display, click any student's mission thumbnail to see advancement. From that point, it's simple to offer comments with the comment feature in Slides or Docs. Use the revision history attribute that is useful to monitor changes. Revision history also lets you observe how successful (or not so successful) a specific pupil was during course time.

The Wave of the Future

Google is all about the cutting edge of technologies and what people today want from systems. An internet-based classroom program permits individuals and schools a platform without having to spend a great deal of cash. The productivity tools that are free offer you a place.

Difference Between Google Classroom and Other Platforms

Let's talk about Google Classroom versus Apple classroom. Google Classroom is the focus of this book, but how does it stack up to Apple classroom? Well, read on to find out.

The Hardware Differences

The biggest difference that you'll run into is the hardware elements. Apple classroom is free for iPad, and essentially, its classroom involves using multiple iPads. Teachers will put these on the device, allowing students to use these as an integrative tool. The teacher's iPad is essentially a collection of these powers, to give a learning experience.

Essentially, it's similar to Google Classroom, and once this is configured, it's connected to devices and the iPad, and shared. Once the session is done, it can be signed out. It's a way to keep students focused, shows students different screens, and it can share documents with the class through the use of

Airdrop. It also shows student work on Apple TV, resets the passwords for students, creates groups of students based on the apps that they use, and allows teachers to create groups and teams. Basically, it's a way to have Apple within the classroom, and through the use of the iPad, it's a collaborative tool within the direct learning atmosphere.

Good for Lower Level Grades

Now, you'll notice immediately, that the only similarity is that Apple Classroom and Google Classroom have the word "classroom" in them. This means, that Apple classroom is more of a direct classroom tool, and it helps teachers show apps and pages to students that might have trouble with this, and show off the work that's there. Teachers benefit from this because it monitors the activity. But the thing is, students can find out if the teacher is watching quickly. It's more of a direct device to use for learning within the classroom. On the other hand, Google Classroom focuses on both in and out of the classroom.

Google Classroom Focuses On Organization

One big part of Google Classroom is the organization element. It is all collaborated with Google Drive, which essentially means that learning based on connections and education is based on organization rather than the classroom setup. Google Classroom makes it easy for teachers to assign the work and allows students to have a better organization of assignments It allows them to get updates faster. It also allows them to go paperless too, which is a big plus. Google Classroom focuses on showing work that needs to be done, any grades that they have, and any assignments that they missed. It's more of a tool fir better organization of the student body, more than anything else.

Google Classroom Allows Multiple Devices To Be Used

Now, you can get the tablets for Google Classroom, but if you want to have students work on something right away, they totally can. The beauty of Google Classroom is that it's not attached to a brand. You can get Google on your computers, and installing chrome is super easy. With that, you are given way more options on using this. Google Classroom can be downloaded as an app on our device, meaning that if you've got a phone or tablet, you're essentially free to use this. This is what is so nice about it, because students can work on assignments right away, and from there, submit it to the teacher. It also allows students to work on different subjects on the go, and they can share different questions and resources with the teacher. It is much more interactive and is perfect for if you have a classroom with multiple smart devices.

The problem with Apple is that it's a brand. You're essentially working only with Apple brand which is highly limited. After all, not everyone may have a Mac or an iPad, so it doesn't really have as much use as Google Classroom does.

You Don't Have to Choose

The reality is that there are some key differences between Apple and Google Classroom, and you can choose based on your needs. Apple Classroom focuses more directly in the class environment itself, and Google classroom is based more on workflow and assignments. They're two different tools; comparing them is like comparing apples and oranges, which is a bit different from your average device comparison since it's often pitted against each other in the technology realm. The truth is, you shouldn't have to choose between both of them because some teachers benefit from both. If you really want to make your classroom the best it can be, sometimes the best answer is to add both of these services, since they're both really good at what they do, and they complement each other well. The answer is, you shouldn't choose one or the other. If you want to get both, get both. If the district can handle both, get both. But, if you're a teacher for a younger group of students, Apple classroom works. If you're a teacher for older students, Google Classroom works.

Apple classroom and Google Classroom are two very different types of software, but both of them accomplish the goal of helping children learn better, so that they can use these skills to improve their life and their future learning endeavors/studies that they will embark on.

CHAPTER 2:

How To Set Up Google Classroom

Getting Started with Google Classroom

Google Classroom is a pretty simple service to use. It's a user-friendly app and there are no complexities whatsoever with regards to how to get started with the app. Before you can use Google Classroom, you need to create an account. You can create an account using your personal Google account, school account, or G Suite account.

To get started with account creation, follow the steps below.

Go to *classroom.google.com.*

Once another window opens, click **Go to Classroom.**

Enter your username and fill out other information. Select **Create account.**

Input your password and click **Next.**

Read any message on the screen and click on **Accept.**

Now, if you are using a G Suite account, click **I'm A Student** or **I'm A Teacher.**

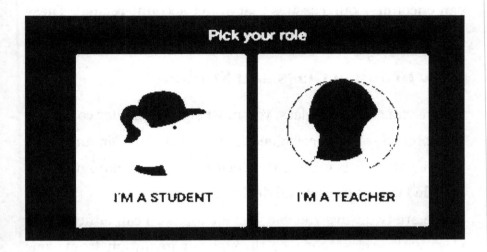

Click on **Get Started**.

You are ready to start using the Google Classroom. You can either create a class (teacher) or join a class (student).

If you signed in as a student, you will see classes that your teachers have created. To see other areas of Google Classroom, click **Menu** (three-lined button). In the **Menu** option, you will see options like:

Classes

Calendar

Work

Settings

Sometimes, you may have trouble signing in. This happens mainly when signing in with the wrong account. However, you can encounter other issues that aren't account-related. These are common signing in mistakes or error messages.

How to Join a Class as a Student

Before you can join a class, you must sign in on your computer or mobile device. Once signed in, then you can join any class. When you join a class on a device, you have automatically enrolled in that class on all devices.

There are two ways you can join a class. You can either join a class with a class code or through an invitation from your teacher.

How to Change Your Profile Picture

You can change your profile picture, update your password, and manage your account settings on the **Settings** page. You can set your display photo next to your name in Google Classroom. As a teacher, your G Suite for Education profile photo is your Classroom profile picture. Once a profile image has been added, you can't remove it. You can only replace it with another photo.

Your photo size file can be up to 5 MB and can be in JPG, JPEG, and PNG file formats. To update your profile picture on your Android smartphone:

Tap the Classroom app.

From the top-left corner of the screen, tap **Menu.**

Scroll down to **Settings** and tap.

Click on Update Photo.

When you are about to set your profile photo, you are given the option to **Take a photo** or **choose a photo**. Choose one, take/upload a photo, tap **Done,** and select **Accept.**

To update your profile picture on your computer:

Go to *classroom.google.com.*

Tap the three parallel lines on the top-left corner.

Scroll down and tap **Settings.**

You will see a profile picture. Click **Change.**

 Settings

Click **Select a photo from your computer.** You can drag a photo from your computer as an alternative.

Click **Set as a profile photo**.

How to Change Password

You can only change your password on a computer. To do that:

Go to *classroom.google.com*.

Tap the **Menu** icon on the top-left corner of your screen.

Scroll to **Settings** and tap.

Under **Account Settings**, select **Manage**.

On the page, you will see **Sign-in & security.** Under it, click **Signing into Google.**

Tap on **Password.**

Input your current password and select **Next.**

Enter your new password.

Verify your password by entering your new password again.

Click **Change Password**.

CHAPTER 3:

How To Organize Topics

Student Topics

While Google Classroom allows each student to attach multiple artifacts during submission of work, they can now submit all the pieces in one place and have it properly organized for the benefit of the teacher.

Projects can be set according to assignment options.

For full class projects, send assignments to the entire class.

You can send assignments to multiple classes by selecting the names of the classes you want to see the assignment, before you send it.

You can send the assignment to certain individuals to create specific student projects.

When creating the assignment, do the following:

Deselect all students.

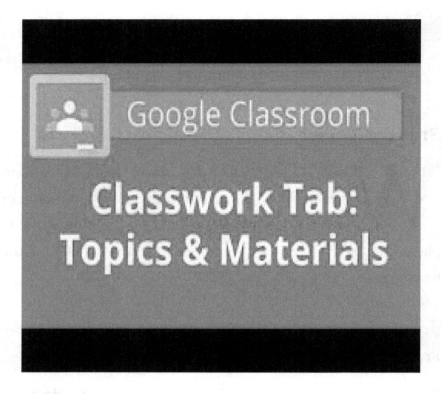

Select the students that you want to be working on the specific project.

Send the assignment.

Only the individual students you selected will receive the assignment.

You can send specific assignments to specific individuals by following the same steps as above.

All the assignments will be organized by students' names, making it easier to keep on top of the assignments and grading.

Google Classroom allows the teachers to create assignments and hand them to students. When working assignments, the teachers are provided with several options. The following steps will help you create an assignment in Google Classroom:

Begin by opening the class in which you need to create the assignment.

On the class page, click the **Classwork** tab located at the top.

You will see a button, **Create**. Click this button.

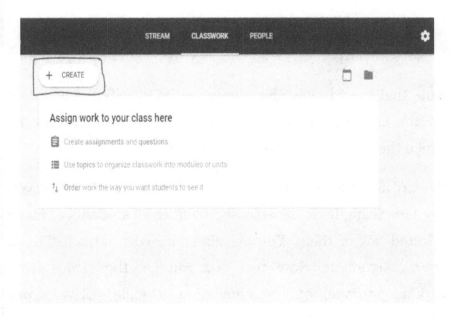

After clicking the button, you will see many options showing the items that you can create for the class. Choose **Assignment**.

A new window will pop up in which you should feed the details for the class. Give a title to the assignment as well as any additional instructions in the next box.

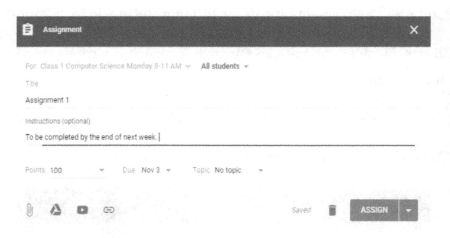

Note that the window also allows you to specify the due date for the assignment as well as the time on the due date by which the assignment should be submitted.

You are also allowed to choose the type of assignment that you need to create. It can be an assignment to all students or just a selected few of them. You are also allowed to attach files to your assignment. Note that you can get these files from various storage options including Google Drive, your computer, etc. The file can also be a video file.

Once you have filled in all the assignment details, click the **Assign** button to assign the assignment to your students. Once the assignment has been created successfully, you will be notified of the same.

In some cases, you may need to assign the assignment to more than one class. In such a case, you only have to click on the class name in the top-left corner of the window and choose all the classes to which you need to assign the work.

Most teachers who use the Google Classroom will prefer to create an assignment from their Drive because this is where most teachers store their resources. However, you will get an advantage when you choose a Drive resource in the Google Classroom, which becomes clear with the options that you get when choosing a file from the Drive:

Students will be able to view the file: You should only choose this option when you need all students to be in a position to view the file but not modify it. It is a good option for generic handouts and study guides that the entire class needs access to.

Students can edit the file: This option should be chosen when you need all students to be able to edit and work on one document. This is good for a collaborative class project in which the students may be working on different slides in a similar Google presentation. It is also applicable in a situation where the students are all brainstorming on an idea collaboratively to discuss in the next class.

Make a copy for each student: When this option is chosen, Google Classroom will make a copy of the file for each student and give them the rights to edit the file. Note that only copies of the original file will be availed to the students, but the teacher's master will remain with him to which the students will not be granted access. This is a good option when you need to distribute a paper with an essay question for students to work on, or where you have a digital worksheet template which you need each student to fill.

You can also view your assignments at any time you want. This is important as you may need to know the assignment details, like the due date. This is possible and it can be done by following the steps given below:

Sign in to your Google Classroom account.

Click the **Menu** button located at the top. Choose Calendar.

You will be taken to a new window with dates. To see either the past or future work, you must use the arrow that is next to **Date**.

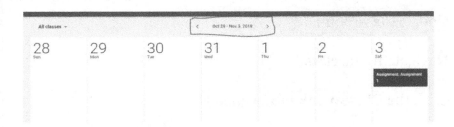

If you need to see all assignments for all your classes, just choose the **All classes** option. If you need to see the assignments for only one class, just click **All classes**, then choose the class for which you need to see the assignments.

Once you identify an assignment or question that you are looking for, just click to open it.

Organizing Assignments

With Google Classroom, one can now organize the assignments based on their topic. This way, you can group the assignments by the unit or classwork from the tab. This is a good way to help students and teachers find the assignment they are looking for more easily.

You can track both your assignments and work using both Google calendar and class calendar. Once a teacher has created an assignment in the classroom, you will be able to see it in both calendars if the account is being used for both calendars.

The following are the steps that will help you create topics in Google Classroom:

Navigate to the class.

Click the **Classwork** tab to open it.

Click the **Create** button.

Select **Topic**.

Give the topic a name and click **Add**.

After creating the topic, you will be notified that students are only allowed to see topics with published posts.

You can now add assignments to the topic from the screen for creating assignments.

You only have to create the drop-down that is located next to the option for the topic.

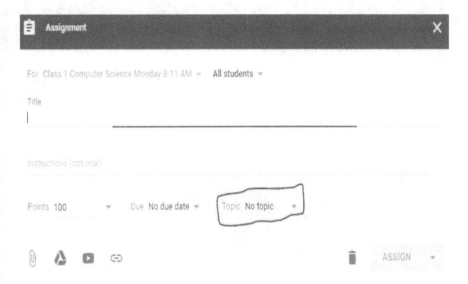

If you have already created the assignment, the following steps will help you assign the assignment to a topic:

Click the **Classwork** tab.

Hover over the assignment that you need to move using your mouse.

Click on **More** (three-dotted button).

Select **Edit**.

Locate the drop-down box that is located next to **Topic**.

Click the drop-down menu, then choose the topic you need to move it to.

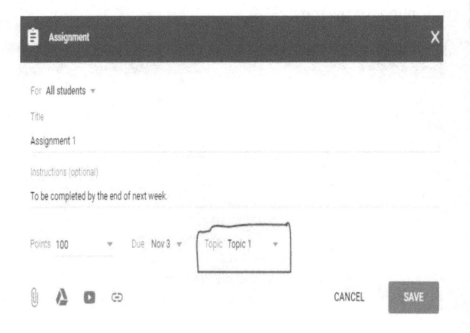

Once you have assigned the assignment to a topic, click the **Save** button to save the changes you have just made.

How Students Access Assignments

When students log into their accounts, they can see their active assignments by clicking and opening the class that they are part of and viewing all their upcoming assignments.

However, there is a quick and easy way to do this.

Just click the **Menu** button located on the top-left corner of the screen then choose **To-do** from the menu that pops out.

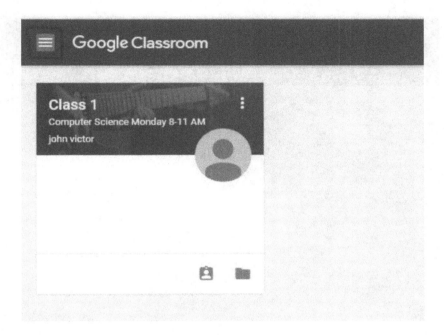

The student will then be able to see all the assignments for his or her classes as well as the ones they have turned in, the outstanding ones, and the overdue ones. The ones that the teacher has graded will be shown alongside their grades.

Once you click on any of the assignments, the relevant file for the student will be opened. If you are dealing with a Google Drive file, an additional button will be added to the toolbar located to the top-right corner and close to the **Share** button. The button will be marked **Turn it in**. Once you click the button, the assignment will be submitted to the teacher. For the regular assignment, you can submit by clicking the **MARK AS DONE** button.

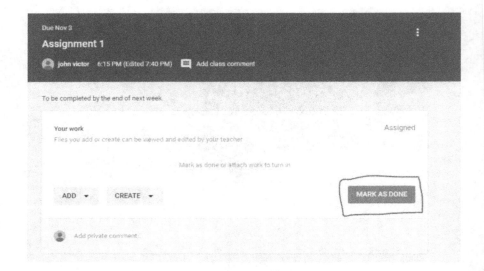

CHAPTER 4:

How To Grade Assignments

Grading Assignments

Google Classroom allows you to hand out graded and ungraded assignments. Graded assignments help the instructor to gauge student understanding of the lessons provided. Just like with regular classrooms, Google Classroom allows the teachers on its platform to grade assignments. It also goes a step forward and allows the teacher to compile the grades in a spreadsheet.

<u>How to Grade Assignments</u>

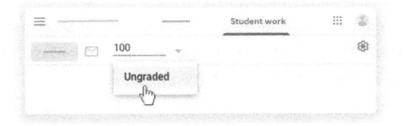

Launch Google Classroom and sign in to your class.

Click on the **Stream** tab.

The assignments you have given out will appear in the column in the center.

Select the assignment you wish to grade.

In the box for **Assignments**, the number of students who have turned in their assignments and the number of those who haven't, will be displayed.

Click on the number of those who have submitted their assignments.

Expand on any student's assignment by clicking on his/her name.

To view the assignment properly, click on the file attached to the assignment. The file will be opened with the corresponding Google App (for instance, Google Docs, Google Sheets, etc.).

Go through the documents and make the necessary input. You can make your comments by using the Comment Tool. Open the Comment tab and insert comments where necessary or highlight the text which you wish to comment on and then select **Insert > Comment**. All comments will be saved in the document.

To allocate grades to the assignment, follow these steps:

Close the document and return to the student's work page under the **Assignment** menu.

Select the option **No Grade.**

Insert a figure for the marks earned. Figures from 1 to 100 are accepted. Letters are, however, not accepted.

Click on the box next to the student's assignment to check it.

Click **Return.** For the assignment to be recorded, it needs to be returned.

You'll be asked to confirm your decision to return the assignment and will be given a chance to provide more feedback.

Provide the feedback (if you wish) and then click on **Return Assignment**.

It is advisable to use Google apps like Google Docs, Google Sheets, etc. because they are already integrated with Google Classroom. Using third-party apps creates the hassle of uploading and downloading files multiple times.

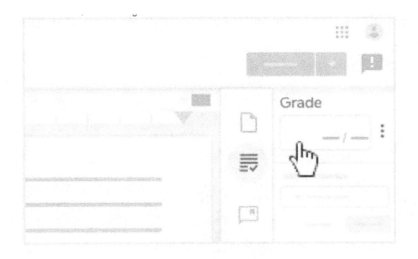

How to Download Grades to Google Sheets

You can export the students' grades in a Comma Separated Values (CSV) file format to Google Sheets. This allows the teacher to study student performance closely. With Google Sheets, you can further analyze the data to find information, such as average scores and so on. Here is how to go about doing this:

Go to your class on Google Classroom. At the top of the screen, select **Classwork**.

Next, click on the assignment the scores of which you wish to export. Click on **View Assignment**.

The **Student Work** page will be displayed. On that page, select **Settings**.

Click on **Copy All Grades to Google Sheets.**

A spreadsheet containing the grades will be created in Google Sheets.

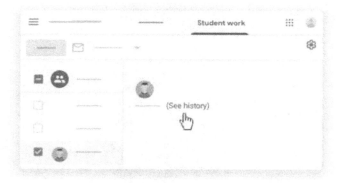

How to Download Grades to a CSV File

You can download the grades as a CSV file which you can use with a spreadsheet software like Microsoft Excel.

You can simply just print the spreadsheet.

Here is how to download students' grades as a CSV file:

Login to your Google Classroom class.

At the top of the screen, select **Classwork**.

Next, click on the assignment whose scores you wish to export.

Click on **View Assignment.**

The Student Work page will be displayed.

On that page, select **Settings**.

Two options will be displayed. You can choose either to:

Download the grades for a single assignment, which appears as **Download these Grades as CSV** button.

Download all grades for the class, which appears as the option **Download all Grades as CSV.**

The file will be saved in your Downloads folder.

You can then use the file to print the grades if you wish.

Setting Rubrics

Rubrics are guides that help you grade assignments. They contain how many points are allocated for each question. With Rubrics in Google Classroom, the rubric score automatically updates as you choose the rating levels. You can only set rubrics with a computer. Sign in to your Google Classroom class.

Go to **Classwork**.

Select the assignment for which you want to set a rubric. Select **View Assignment** and then open the student's file.

On the column to the right click **Grading.**

Assign a rating for each criterion. To use the criterion to score, enter a number.

Grading with Rubrics

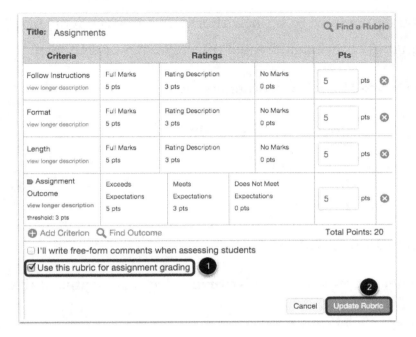

Having set up the rubric for a particular assignment, you can now proceed to use it to grade assignments.

Sign in to your Google Classroom class.

Go to **Classwork**.

Select the assignment and click **View Assignment**.

Select the student's file which will open in the grading tool.

When a column opens on the right-hand side, click **Grading**.

You can view a criterion's description by clicking the arrow buttons (up and down arrows).

<u>Reusing Rubrics</u>

You do not have to set new rubrics for every assignment. You can reuse previously created rubrics on new assignments.

Go to your Google Classroom class.

Select the Class and click on **Classwork**.

Create the assignment.

Click on + **Rubric.**

Select **Reuse Rubric**.

Under the option **Select Rubric**, select an assignment title.

Exporting a Rubric

You can export your rubric so that other teachers may use it to grade their students. In the same way, you can also import rubrics from other teachers to grade your students.

Go to your Class.

Select **Classwork.**

Select the assignment which has the rubric you want to share or export.

In the upper-right corner, select **More**.

Click on **Export to Sheets**.

Go to the Classwork page.

Select the Class Drive Folder.

Click on **My Drive**.

You will see the Rubric Exports folder containing all exported rubrics.

You can either select individual files and share them or share the entire folder.

You share by right-clicking the file/folder and clicking **Share.**

Enter the recipient's name or email address.

Click on **Send**.

Importing a Rubric Shared with You

Here is how to import rubrics other teachers share with you.

On your Google Classroom home page, click **Classwork.**

Select **Create.**

Click **Assignment** and enter a title for the assignment.

Click **Add Rubric.**

Select **Import from Sheets**.

The folder containing imported sheets will be opened.

Select the rubric you wish to import and click **Add**.

Click **Save**.

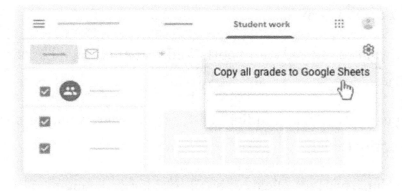

Grading Tips

Let me answer some of the questions that you may be asking yourself as far as grading students is concerned:.

Once a teacher has returned an assignment to the student, the teacher no longer has editing rights of the assignment document.

You can return an assignment to a student without grading it by checking the box located to the left of the student name, and clicking the **RETURN** button. This is important and useful for assignments that have been submitted erroneously.

After returning an assignment, the student gets an email notification about the same.

You are allowed to change the student's grade anytime you want by clicking the grade, then typing in the new grade. Note that this should be done within the same box in which we first entered the student grade.

If you click the folder button, you will be able to open the Google Drive folder in which all the assignments from students have been stored. This can help you when you need to view all the submitted assignments at once.

By default, each assignment has a total of 100 points, but this can be changed when clicking on the drop-down arrow. Then choose another value or simply type a value of your own. You can also select the option of not scoring the assignment.

CHAPTER 5:

Cancellation of a Course

How to Remove, Delete and View a Class

When using Google Classroom, sometimes you'll want to delete a class when it's the end of the semester, and you can always restore it again if you need to.

You can also delete it if you never want to see that class again or have no use for it because you've got the assignments already.

Now, if you don't archive these, they will stick around, so make sure that you archive them first.

Archived classes essentially are in an area where you have the same materials and posts the work students have.

You can view it, but you can't actually use it, and this is good if a student wants the materials.

Archiving classes is simple to do.

You choose the class, press the three-dotted button, and presto! It's archived.

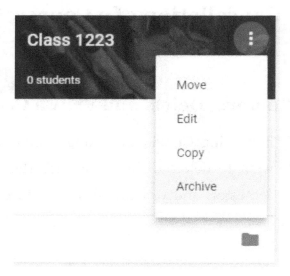

Now to view an archived class after it's been archived, you press the three-lined button again. Go down to the tab that says archive classes, and then choose the class you want to see.

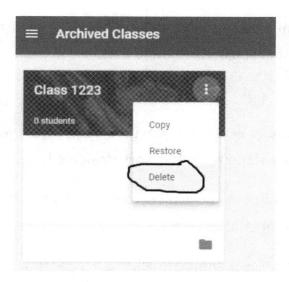

To delete a class, though, you essentially need to do the same thing.

Remember, that you need to archive the class before you can delete it; so, scroll down, choose archive classes. Once you have the classes, press the three dotted button, and then choose to **Delete This**.

From there, the class will be fully removed. Remember though, you can't undo this once you've done it, and if you do choose to delete a class, you don't have access to the comments or the posts.

But if you have any files that are in the Drive, you can always access those, since you have those in the class files themselves.

Remove A Student From A Class

•Go to *classroom.google.com*.

•Click **People**.

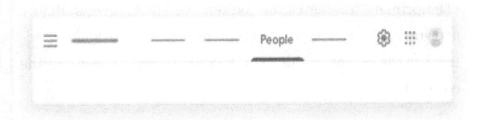

•Tick the box that is next to the student that you want to remove.

•At the top, click **Actions > Remove**.

•Click **Remove** to confirm.

Remove A Teacher From A Class

A primary teacher and/or co-teacher can remove another co-teacher from a class.

Before you begin.

•The primary teacher cannot be removed from a class. Before a primary teacher leaves a class, he/she has to make a co-teacher the owner of the class, before leaving the class to the co-teacher.

Remove a co-teacher

1. Go to *classroom.google.com.*

2. Click the class **People**.

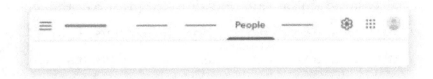

3. Next to the co-teacher's name, click **More** > **Remove**.

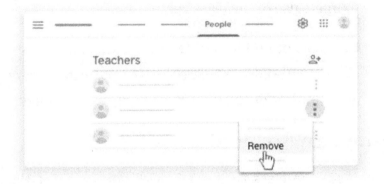

4. Click **Remove** to confirm.

Delete a Class

You can archive a class when you're done teaching it. A class is archived for all students and teachers in the class when it is archived. Students and teachers in a class will continue to see a class on their **Classes** page if you don't archive it.

A primary teacher can delete a class while teachers and co-teachers can only archive it. Students on the other hand can't archive or delete a class.

What happens to an archived class?

- It's saved in a safe location to preserve the class materials, work, and posts of the students. It won't be displayed in your active classes on the **Classes** page.

- The primary teacher and the students can still view an archived class. You have to restore the class if you want to make use of the class again.

- The teacher and his students can still gain access to any class materials in Google Drive. Attachments for assignments or other student work are included.

Restore An Archived Class

You can see the class card again with your current classes if you restore an archived class. You can reuse its comments, assignments, posts, and materials again.

1. Go to *classroom.google.com*.

2. At the top, click **Menu**.

3. Scroll down and click **Archived Classes**.

Note: This option won't be available on the menu if you haven't archived any classes.

CHAPTER 6:

The Teacher's View

Getting started with the class is ending up being more and more paperless. Instructors have to begin finding services to hand out tasks, manage their class, interact with trainees, and so on, without meeting physically. The very first time a teacher enters Google Classroom, he/she will be asked to suggest if he is a student or an instructor. To begin, the teacher will locate, in the upper ideal hand corner of Google Classroom, a plus button (+) to allow the instructor to **Join class** or **Create class**.

Clicking **Create class** creates a tile in Google Classroom and sets up a folder in the instructor's Google Drive. The teacher might opt to have students from different areas enroll in the same class. Trainees do not have the option of **Create class**. Students can be welcomed to a class from the **Students** tab in Google Classroom.

Google Classroom is a closed environment. Only trainees who have signed up with or were invited to join Google Classroom can view the announcements and assignments. This enables students' comments and names to stay personal.

Teacher Overview

Stream

The Stream is where trainees can view projects and statements published to Google Classroom.

Classmates

Using the **Classmates** icon, students can sight a list of the other trainees enrolled in the Google Classroom.

About

The **About** tab shows any information the instructor has posted about the class. Resources, such as the curriculum and other files relating to the class, however, are not tasks, but may be found in the **About** tab for students to find quickly.

Share

Students can connect files, links, or Google Drive files to the stream in their remark. Teachers can silence a trainee's capability to do this from the **Students** tab.

Menu

Trainees can switch classes, return to the primary menu, or see a list of their projects in the upper-left corner using the **Menu** tab.

Announcements

Documents posted by the instructor as announcements are produced as "view only for students. Trainees can read the statement and open attached files or links in the announcement.

Add Comment

Unless silenced by the instructor, trainees can publish a reaction or concern to any announcement or project. Students can't attach files to the announcement.

Assignment

Students can find tasks the teacher has posted in the stream, after they gain access to links or accessories in the task directly from the stream. Project template files provided by the teacher are not visible in the stream. Design templates are found on the task submission screen.

Open

For each project, an **Open** button is offered. Trainees click on the **Open** button to expose the project submission screen. If the instructor has picked to offer a design template for part of the assignment, the design template documents distributed to the students are offered.

Discussed next are a few things the teachers can do in the Classroom.

Add an Announcement

Here's a fantastic way to interact with the class and keep them updated about the information. All announcements are posted to the Class Stream, but no grade is associated with it. Go to the Class Stream, then click on **Share something with your class**. Now you are free to add the text for the announcement.

This is the place where a student can work. The teachers can create a graded or ungraded question that should be answered by students. You, as a teacher, can do it under the **Classwork** tab. It is also possible to attach materials for your class or even reuse an old post.

Things to include in the question or assignment:

A comprehensive title for your assignment.

A description. It helps the students to recall and refer back to the assignment later.

Points. Select how many points or marks the assignment or question carries (or you can use the dropdown menu to upgrade it).

A due date. It is possible to choose the submission date (don't use a due date).

A topic. You can see more under the number 3.

File attachments. Assign the assignment right away, schedule to post it later (it will be done automatically), or you can save an assignment as a draft to complete it later.

CHAPTER 7:

The Student View

Connecting to Classroom For The First Time

When you log in to Classroom for the first time:

Log in to Classroom at *classroom.google.com*. with your Google Apps for Education account.

Click on **Student**. The "Welcome to Classroom" page is displayed with the message "Enter code to participate in the course." The teacher tells you the course code. Enter the course code and click participates.

For more information about participating in a course, see the **Add a course** page.

To access the other Classroom areas listed below, click the three-lined button in the upper-left corner, and proceed as shown:

- Homework: You can view all homework associated with your classes (upcoming homework, as well as homework completed and corrected by the teacher).

- Course files: You can view the materials of all your homework.

- Settings: You can manage your Classroom preferences, such as your password, security options, and access to other Google services. For more information, see the change **Account Settings** page.

Participate in A Course

The teacher can either invite you to a course or provide you with a code allowing you to join the course yourself. If you are invited to a course, log in to Classroom at *classroom.google.com.*, then click the **Participate** button associated with the course. If you receive an invitation to a course you don't want to participate in, sign into the Classroom, and click the deny button associated with the course.

To add yourself to a course using the corresponding code:

Log in to Classroom at *classroom.google.com.*

View homework You can view homework in the course stream, as well as on the **Homework** page. The **Homework** page allows you to sort your homework by status ("to do" or "completed") and by course. You can also view the assignments that have been scored and rendered.

Possibility to put comments when the student hands over his homework to the teacher:

Post a message in a course Stream.

You can publish a message in a class stream at any time.

Log in to Classroom at *classroom.google.com.*

Select the course to open the corresponding stream.

Click the **Share with your class** box at the top of the page and enter your message.

Find and select the desired item, then click **Add**. If you want to attach a link, enter the corresponding text, and click **Add**. As soon as you add the item, it appears in the message. If you choose not to use the attachment, click the **X** button to the right to remove it.

If you choose not to post the message, click the trash icon at the bottom to delete it.

When you're done, click **Post**.

All students in the course can comment on your message. They simply click in the **Add comment** box, enter their message, and click post. All comments are visible in the feed, under the ad. You can edit or delete comments by clicking the menu icon (three-dotted button) in the upper-right corner of the comment, and clicking **Edit** or **Delete**.

To edit or delete an ad, click the **Menu** icon (three-dotted button) in the upper-right corner of the ad, and select **Edit Message** or **Delete Message**.

Send an Email

To send an email to a teacher:

Log in to Classroom at *classroom.google.com*.

Click on the course of the teacher you want to send an email to.

In the top banner, click the envelope icon next to the teacher's name.

A copywriting window appears. Enter your message and its subject, then click **Send**.

To send an email to another student:

Log in to Classroom at *classroom.google.com*.

Click on the course of the student to whom you want to send an email.

Click the **Classmates** tab.

To the right of the student's name, click the envelope icon.

A copywriting window appears. Enter your message and its subject, then click **Send**.

<u>Mark a Task As Complete</u>

To mark a homework assignment as complete in Classroom:

Log in to Classroom at *classroom.google.com.*

Go to the course flow or click the **Main menu** icon in the upper-left corner and select homework to access the list of your homework.

In the course stream, homework appears in the order of their assignment. You can click the show all button in the **Homework** area on the left, to view the homework of this course on the **homework** page.

Click on the task you want to mark as complete.

Click **Add** to access an existing document in Google Drive, attach a link, or import a file from your computer. Find and select the desired item, then click **Add**. If you want to attach a link, enter the appropriate link text, and click **Add link**. When you add the item, the item appears in the assignment. If you choose not to use the attachment, click the **X** button to the right to remove it.

If you want to change your assignment after marking it as complete:

Log in to Classroom at *classroom.google.com.*

Go to the course flow or click the **Main menu** icon in the upper-left corner and select homework to access the list of your homework.

In the course stream, homework appears in the order of their assignment. You can click the **Show All** button in the **Homework** area on the left, to view the homework of this course on the **Homework** page.

Click the task to edit it.

Click the **Cancel Bid** button and click **Cancel bid** again. The duty then takes the state "not completed." So, you need to think about resubmitting it before its deadline.

Make any necessary changes and import the required new documents and links.

Click the **Reset** or **MARK AS DONE** button.

If so, add a private comment for the teacher, and click **Reset** or **MARK AS DONE**.

All assignments marked as completed after their due date are set to "late."

View a graded assignment

You can view homework scored by a teacher on the homework page or in the class feed.

View An Assignment Noted In The Course Stream

Log in to Classroom at *classroom.google.com.*

Select the course to open the corresponding stream.

Search for the assignment in the course stream and click **Open**.

To view the assignments associated with this course on the **Homework** page, click the show all button in the **Homework** area on the left.

Unsubscribe from a course

The teacher can remove you from a course, or you have the option to unsubscribe yourself.

To unsubscribe from a course:

Log in to Classroom at *classroom.google.com.*

On the homepage, click on the other actions icon (three-dotted button) in the upper-right corner of the course sheet you want to leave. Click **Unsubscribe**.

If you unsubscribe from a course, you will be removed from the course. You will no longer be able to view or comment on the feed. However, you will still be able to access your documents through Google Drive.

A Student's View: Announcements & Questions

All the announcements will appear in the student's Stream and are usually read-only; however, if the instructor has allowed this, students have the choice to make a class statement. The teacher and all students that are part of the class can watch class posts. The students may also access the data, connections, or clips if the announcement has any attachments.

A Student's View of Questions in the Stream

Once the students are given a topic for discussion, it should be instantly shown in the Stream. Students are going to see the below stream options:

Final state (not finished or accomplished)

Deadline Date (Students can even see if the assignment given is late)

Name and Summary of discussion

Your response: This is where participants put in their answers. Students must first send their answers before they can access the answers from other classmates.

<u>Add a Class Message:</u> Use this room to ask difficult questions or to reply to other's inquires. It is NOT where you type in your answers to the questions provided by your instructor.

<u>*Note:*</u> The question's heading is clickable and will transfer students to a specific page for that topic. Students may also choose to put in their answer on this tab, but they will now have the opportunity to make a personal message, which the instructor can only access. Make sure students comprehend to enter their answers in the answer reply field, and not comment as well as personally reply.

Share Resources

Google Classroom lets teachers take a file, video, or link and push it out to their students. Using Google Classroom as a consistent location for users to acquire electronic resources maximizes the time required for classroom teaching. The classroom environment is improved when students are not driven to different places to locate the required resources.

Click the **Announcement** button at the top of the Google Classroom Stream to share your resource. There are four icons at the bottom edge of the creation box for announcements.

The paper clip symbol attaches saved files on to the computer.

The Google Drive icon requires the announcement to be added to the announcement from Google Docs or any files saved in the Google Drive of the teacher. If the file is stored personally in Google Drive, the sharing settings are changed to allow students to access the file without the instructor taking any further action.

Create a Lesson

Google Classroom enables the instructor to construct a comprehensive lecture, rather than simply assigning tasks to the students. The teacher may click on **Assignment** at the top of the Classroom Stream to start creating a lesson series. The assignment's summary area enables the instructors to give students instructions for finishing the lesson and its related assignment.

Students can move more effectively through the lecture when the resources and materials are provided in a logical sequence. The lesson set may be started by making and adding an instructional file on Google Drive by using the Google Drive symbol.

CHAPTER 8:

Students Approach Ideas

J ust__like students in real-life classrooms need motivation now and again, your students on Google Classroom will need to be motivated regularly, so that they interact and give their best to the lessons. Here are a few trusted tips to get your students motivated and engaged in your classroom.

Teachers and educators can get quite a bit out of Google Classroom to organize their students and make their teaching more effective. They are allowed to monitor all of their students in one area, keeping classes separate, making announcements, and doing so much more to help students learn, so they can spend more time teaching rather than spending so much time on their regular administrative tasks.

Students can also benefit from Google Classroom. While the students will not be able to add people to the class and are limited on the resources they can upload onto the platform, there are plenty of opportunities for them to interact with each other, communicate with the teacher, and learn in new ways!

Logging In

At the beginning of the school year, your teacher will be able to invite you to join their classroom. You will simply need to give them a preferred email and then accept the invitation and link that they send to you later on. This will allow you access to the Classroom, and you can see all the announcements and assignments that the teacher gives for that year. You can also stream content, read materials, take tests and quizzes, partake in discussions, and hand in homework assignments all in one place. Make sure that the email address you provide is one you use often, otherwise, you could miss out on some of the important information needed to do well in class. Consider signing up for a Gmail account that is only for school and giving that to each teacher who uses Google Classroom. This allows all your school announcements to be in one place and limits the chance that something gets lost in another email address.

Sharing

Students are allowed to share their thoughts and opinions in Classroom. By going to the Stream tab, you can provide an answer to discussion questions the teacher posts, and the whole class will be able to see. You can attach supporting documents to this as well including videos, weblinks, files, and documents. This is separate from where you would do tests or essays and other homework. The Stream tab is a place where others will be able to see your information and what you have posted, and can even comment on it themselves. If you are doing a discussion question or you have found something interesting to share with the whole class, this is the option for you. If you are sending in a homework assignment or a test, you will use Google Forms or Drive to get this done.

Assignments

Your teacher will be able to upload assignments onto Classroom for everyone to see. Rather than printing papers and expecting students to remember each assignment from multiple classes each day, Classroom allows the students to get into their class and find all the information needed for the assignment. To see your assignments, you simply need to click on the button **View All** to see a list of assignments for a particular class. You can see To-Do items, such as if you need to read a document before starting or a reminder for a test. Students have the option to mark whether an assignment is done. Many assignments will require a link or file to complete. For example, if a student needed to write out an essay or submit answers to a discussion question, they may have written the answers in Word outside of Classroom. In these cases, the assignment feature allows students to upload these links. Students can also comment on an assignment but remember that others in the class will be able to see these comments. If a student has a question about an assignment, they can simply email the teacher through their Gmail account. The teacher can then respond personally to the student, without notifying the whole class, and get the questions answered promptly.

Organization

Classroom is hooked to Google Calendar so students can look at their assignments, test dates, and other important information and find out when everything is due at a glance. This can help students to keep track of their assignments and makes it easier to plan out how to get all the work done. In Calendar, students can change the color to match with the class, and they can set up text message alerts to remind them of upcoming due dates on assignments.

Feedback

Google Classroom allows students to discuss various parts of their homework and tests with the teacher. In a regular classroom setting, the student will submit the work, the teacher will grade it with a few comments, and that is the end. There isn't enough time in class for the student to discuss the grade or comment, and many may not be able to bring up this discussion later. With Classroom, the student can leave a comment under feedback from the teacher, and a discussion can begin that helps the student understand why they got a certain grade or even clarify their answers.

This allows for more discussion and learning than what may go on in the traditional classroom.

Discussion Time

Many teachers like the feature of adding discussion questions inside Classroom. These discussion questions allow students to talk about a particular topic and learn together in a setting that is more comfortable than speaking in the classroom. Sometimes the teacher may not have time for a full discussion in class and other times; this is a tool used to bring shy students out to speak their opinions. Either way, students are learning from each other, considering different ideas, and gaining more knowledge easily.

Google Apps

Google has many great apps to use, and all of them are free. This makes it easy for students to get on and use everything that is needed on the platform. Through Google Classroom, students can enjoy other apps including Google Calendar, Google Spreadsheets, Docs, Presentation, Gmail, Drive, and much more. These are great tools that can help students out at any level of education, even if their class is not using Classroom at the time. Students will become familiar with using these apps on the platform and seeing what a difference they make in learning and presenting themselves.

Functions and Benefits of Classroom to Students

There are so many great benefits to students using Google Classroom. While many times the focus is on the teacher and how they will be able to streamline their teaching process and help students learn more, students are getting some of the best benefits out of this tool. They are opening up to new ideas, finding creative ways to learn, and even having more of teachers' attention than in a traditional classroom.

Some of the other benefits that students can enjoy using Classroom include:

- If a particular lesson is not clear to the student, they can add feedback and save the lesson to a new folder for revisions later once clarification is done.

- Students can privately ask their teacher a question.

- The ability to create and also monitor how they are doing in a particular class using Google Sheets.

- Ability to email either individual students or a group of students and start up a conversation. This can be helpful in discussions when missing a day in school, or for a project.

- Students can submit their assignments as attachments in many forms including links, videos, files, and voice clips.

- Reduce how much paper is used in the classroom.

- Fewer missed due dates, since they have all their homework in one place and can monitor them on Google Calendar at a glance.

- Shy students can reply to questions online and engage without being worried about talking in front of other people. This allows for more engagement out of the class and for everyone to be heard.

- Students can use Google Classroom on their smartphones, making it easier to receive notifications and work on assignments anywhere.

- It is easy for students to work together, even outside of class, and for teachers to provide feedback and comments on assignments, so students learn more than ever.

- Better organization allows students to keep all the information for one class in one place. This limits the likelihood of losing an assignment, forgetting about it, or leaving the paper at home. Students can simply log on to their Classroom and complete homework assignments, tests, and more, in one location.

- Instant feedback is allowed. Taking tests can be hard, but it is nice to get instant feedback. Your teacher can choose an add-on that provides instant feedback on test scores and some types of homework, allowing you a chance to see how you did right away, rather than waiting a week or more for the teacher to have time to grade all the papers.

CHAPTER 9: **Cha**

pter 9: How To Increase Student Engagement With Google Classroom By Teaching Activities

E ven most well-intending students can be distracted when they should pay attention. The delay when it's time to log in and do their classwork.

Training Instructors in Online Learning

Many instructors are subject matter experts but are not trained in adult education or online learning.

You can't simply transfer a learning experience in-person to an online platform.

The curriculum, content and course delivery must be specifically designed for online learning. An online instructor needs to understand not only how students learn, but also how to harness technology to help them assimilate and retain information.

Plan the Diversity of Deliveries

Bring instructors and guest speakers, so they don't tire of seeing the same face and hearing the same voice.

Be a Storyteller

Storytelling has been a buzzword in recent years. But, like all clichés, it has permanent power because it is based on facts. We love beautiful stories, the emphasis on good. We love reading or listening to stories that we can relate to in some way. Stories exploit emotions so that we can remember the information provided in the stories.

If you are reading something difficult, you are more likely to "catch" if the writer uses an example to illustrate what he is trying to convey. The case studies are based on one of the oldest stories: the hero's journey. Watch the dragon (problem) and our hero (the student proxy), watch the hero kill the dragon (solution), and see what happens next (hit).

Engage students by stopping the story from finding out what they would do instead of the hero. Or show the same story from alternative perspectives, if this is important for the learning outcome.

Set Due Dates for Assignments

The due dates for assignments usually provide extra motivation for students compared to assignments without due dates. Due dates motivate students to get the work done and not keep on procrastinating. Set reasonable due dates for assignments given.

This will motivate students to get the work done.

Setting due dates is easy:

Create the Assignment

Type in the title, instructions, and upload any attachments, if need be.

On the right-hand side of the panel, there is a tab for **Due Date.**

Click on the tab and select a due date for the assignment.

Click on **Create.**

Use private comments to give and receive feedback.

Google Classroom has the Private Comment feature which allows you to make comments on student work and give feedback on their performance. This is important because it provides a clear path for confidential two-way communication.

You can use this feature to directly motivate students, by giving helpful comments and encouraging them to perform better. Nothing motivates a student more than encouragement and praise from a teacher. Praise students in private comments when necessary to motivate them to do better. Private comments can be referred to at any time; hence, help students to remember your helpful comments.

Here's how private comments are added from the **Student Work** page:

Start at the **Classwork** tab; select the assignment on which you want to make a private comment.

Click **View Assignment**.

Select the student whose work you wish to comment on from the roster on the left of the screen.

Click on the **Add Private Comment** button. It is at the bottom of the right-hand panel.

Click on it to type your comment.

You can also make private comments while grading students' assignments. Follow these steps to add private comments as you grade assignments:

Start at the **Classwork** tab. Click on the assignment you want to give a private comment on.

Click **View Assignment**.

Select the student's file you would want to comment on.

Use the panel on the right side of the screen to post a comment.

Add Quizzes to Make Things More Fun

You can create quizzes on your Google Classroom environment. Quizzes provide a source for added engagement. They can motivate the students to learn in a fun way as well. Creating Quizzes is easy to do within the Google Classroom environment.

Login to Google Classroom.

Select the Class and then click on **Classwork**.

Click on **Create** and select **Quiz Assignment**.

Type in the title and instructions for the quiz.

Turn on **Grade Importing** if you wish to import the quiz grades.

You will also have to make settings to determine:

Whether the quiz is to be posted to one or more classes

If it will be posted to individual students

The grade categories

Point values

The topics

Due dates

You can lock the quiz and prevent your students from leaving the quiz page while they take the quiz. This feature is open to only Chromebooks managed by the school. With the locked mode, students can't use browsers while the quiz is on. The teacher will be notified when a student closes the quiz and reopens it. Simply turn on Locked Mode by toggling it when setting up the quiz.

Gamify the Environment

Apart from quizzes, games are a good way to keep your students engaged and motivated. The type of games you integrate into the classroom depends on the age of the students and what class you are teaching. Generally, gamifying the environment brings fun to the class.

There are hundreds of game apps you can integrate into the classroom. They are integrated into Google Classroom just like the other apps. Examples of game apps that make Google Classroom exciting are Classcraft, Bookwidget, Quizziz, Kahoot, FlipQuiz, and BrainPop.

Using Private Comment to Get Students to Reflect

A good way to get students to be more motivated is to go beyond routine communication and ask students questions that make them reflect on assignments. Using private comments, you can ask students to reflect on given assignments and respond with profound knowledge they have discovered. This motivates students to carry out tasks, not just to get them done, but to learn something new as well.

Assign Successful Coaches

Provide online learning and study tips.

Successful coaches take their online learning program to the next level. This added value is not predictable, but it shows that your association is investing in the professional growth of students.

Online learning can be a lonely experience. The more you can personalize it by connecting in some way with students, the more likely they are to remain engaged and become avid fans.

Coaches can proactively reach students to specific course milestones.

Encourage Responsibility

Take advantage of the email notification feature in your learning management system. Schedule and send automatic emails to students who do not log in for a certain number of days or who do not complete an assignment on time. Alternatively, you can configure it so that the instructor receives a notification and personally communicates with students to see what happens to them.

These records are also a good time to receive comments.

Study groups can also act as reminders of responsibility, just like meeting friends in the gym. Students must also experience a sense of internal responsibility. You can help with this.

Help Students Cultivate Intrinsic Motivation

Extrinsic motivators, like digital certificates and badges, show others what you know and what you can do. Intrinsic motivators push a person forward.

They should know that what they are doing here is essential. Talk about how this unique experience enables you to improve or contribute to your company, industry, or profession, or how it affects your clients or customers.

Your association's efforts to improve the learning experience show students that you care about their growth and success. As students become more involved in the learning experience, they will benefit more from the course and are more likely to return to you for further education.

CHAPTER 10:

Extension Apps

Insert Learning Extensions

This is an extension that allows you to convert webpages to interactive class lessons. This extension will allow you to add sticky notes, links, videos, quizzes, and questions for discussion to the webpage, and share with your students on Google Classroom. It is a great extension that will help you make your lessons more interactive and keep the students motivated.

Google Cast for Education

This is a Chrome app that lets students and tutors share screens wirelessly. With this app, teachers can control who can be added to view the screens and can add students from Google Classroom.

Alice Keeler's Classroom Split

This is an extension by Alice Keeler that splits the Chrome screen. It allows students to view assignment instructions and work on the assignment side by side.

That way they do not need to keep on shuttling between tabs or minimizing and maximizing constantly.

Google Classroom Apps

Several apps that integrate with Google Classroom do so through the **Share** button.

While some of these apps connect seamlessly for free, you may have to pay to integrate some.

The steps in integrating an app with Google Classroom are outlined below:

Open an account on the app or log in to your account if you have one.

Create the resource or activity you want to bring to Google classroom or locate a resource or activity you have already created.

Click on the **Share to Classroom** button.

The first time you click on it, you will be asked to grant permission to the app to connect to your Google Classroom account.

This connection will allow you to share special content on the app to your Google Classroom and share it as an assignment, announcement, or question.

Writable

Develop extraordinary writers with this guided work on including adjustable assignments and Google Classroom mix.

Pearson Education

Incorporates with G Suite™ for Education to share substance, appraisals, and lists with a single sign-on.

Assessments

Offers input to instructors and students synchronously when students total assignments utilizing this free online device.

Effectively Learn

Assist students in building literacy abilities with write-ups and activities that energize comprehension and maintain an assortment of subjects.

Addition App

Effectively oversee everyday classroom activities and correspondence, and exercise arranging and tracking student progress with this digital grade book and classroom organizer.

Aeries

Upgrade your educational plan with the board programming arrangements that permit you to make new Classroom classes, import student scores into Aeries, etc.

Aeries Student Information System

Oversee and track grades, test scores, and participation. Effectively share data with students and guardians.

That's only the tip of the iceberg.

Aladdin

Improve school organization with simple-to-get information, electronic participation records, and arranging and detailing instruments.

Alma

Get clear experiences of student execution, track participation, modify evaluating rubrics, and discuss consistently with students and guardians.

Aristotle Insight K12

Engage students to become wise and safe digital citizens with this across-the-board classroom that enables content separating and detailing arrangement.

Book Widgets

Move from paper tests to intelligent tests and worksheets. You can redo these for your classroom with programmed evaluating, to spare you time.

BrainPOP

Draw in students with a wide scope of subjects with more than 1,000 educational plans. They include enlivened films, intelligent activities and energetic games.

Assorted VR Apps

Virtual reality is super popular these days, to the point where Google Classroom has a couple of apps on it. But here are the best VR apps to use.

Animal flashcards are a great way to use VR with flashcards, allowing children to learn about various animals, and also learn the letters easier. It's a unique app, and you get realistically rendered animals to look at. You can tap the image to hear the name and the letters that are in the name of the animal. Quiver is a coloring app made for learning. It's based on VR, which means that you can color some interesting characters with this technology, view cool animals, play interactive games, and even get quizzes and facts on it.

Skill-Building Apps

For students who need a bit of help organizing their lives and homework, Studious is the answer to this. It's a homework planner that allows students to organize and improve their ability to keep track of everything. You'll get reminders of when assignments are due, when tests are coming up, and you can even take notes and send emails. It is great because you can scan and print documents from your phone, create a personal assignment calendar, organize your assignments to be prepared, and edit your courses and such, giving you a chance to improve your ability to understand classes.

CHAPTER 11:

How To Save Time In Your Work

Re-Order Classes

Your classes are the easiest to see in the order you teach them. You can now rearrange the tiles for each of your courses in an order that works for you! Do this by a simple drag-and-drop action. Alternatively, press the three dotted button in the top-right corner of the class card and select **Switch**.

Move Class Ownership Often

Mid-year changes occur, and now teachers and administrators have the option of transferring ownership of current Google Classroom files and property of all associated Classroom files. For example, a long-term replacement began the school year last year by building a classroom. When a permanent teacher returned, the only choice for children to continue working in the same class was to add a permanent teacher as a co-teacher to hold the account open for the replacement who had left. The upgrade would make it easier for teachers and schools to respond to changes while preserving the current Classroom.

Keeping Kids Involve While at Home

Digital learning can isolate and disengage students. Watching videos for hours on end may force them to skim through or skip lessons. To keep them interested, have virtual conversations about the lessons they are studying. On the topic of the water cycle, for example, have students pause the video and discuss via Stream on their latest thunderstorm experience. Another way to engage them is through Classroom and Google Docs, where you can have a dialogue as you give comments on their outputs.

Frequent Assessment of Student Learning

Formative tests help you ensure that students continue to develop even at home. Test for comprehension during community teaching by polling them during the presentation of a particular lesson and presenting the results instantaneously. It will surely help them take part in a virtual world. You can also auto-grade their exams through the Quizzes feature in Google Forms.

This way, you can add videos, photos, and other important materials. You may also employ graded discussions, and observe students demonstrating their expertise through assignments that can be presented through slides or Docs.

Use Hangouts Meet for Further Engagements

When there is an interruption on students' routine, they will start to miss their usual structured schedule and being around with fellow students and teachers. In a time of uncertainty, it is necessary to retain this sense of comfort and protection.

You can connect with your students via Hangouts Meet if they have access to Wi-Fi. Through this platform, you can create video discussions so students can interact and help their colleagues who may have difficulty with concepts. Switch on the captions so students can concentrate and follow the discussion thread by reading these captions.

Monitor How Your Students Feel

The students' emotional and social learning has to go on even at a distance. In the same way, you can use Hangouts Meet to be present for your students and preserve the atmosphere of your Classroom, and you can also provide the students with other ways to express their feelings while at home. Creating mood check-ins on Google Forms can help you assess your students' state of emotions every day. Google Forms features a request for the private conference if the students feel the need to talk with you in private. You can also have a blog that will guide the students by encouraging them to journal or record videos of their reflections.

Think Beyond Time

Distance learning spares you from the time limitations of a regular day, which usually involves students rushing into classrooms or teachers hurrying through the lessons before the bell rings. With Google Classroom, students can work at their pace and do other things and learn lessons naturally. Make the most of this chance and expand your experiences through "choose your adventure" type activities instead of a set lecture and lesson schedule.

Find Other Ways of Distance Learning

Administrators and teachers may need to work on contingencies and consider setting up fully virtual classrooms. With the use of Google Educator Groups, Twitter, or Facebook, school administrators and leaders have been conferring with one another on this particular matter.

Google Classroom Bolsters

Using Google Classroom, teachers can carry their papers in a single dashboard for all their lessons. Just a few clicks, you can allocate homework to every Classroom digitally.

Google Classroom makes the work of educators simpler as it prevents travel to the copier.

"With Google Classroom, students have immediate feedback, and the instructor may evaluate in depth the questions have

been answered properly or wrongly by which students," writes McKenney. *"The teacher can see areas at a glance that need reteaching or clarification."* Students who skip classes can quickly catch up on the assignments using a web-based classroom.

Ease IT Workflow

Google Classroom is also ideal for managers and IT teams. Alerts inform them when suspicious activities happen. Teachers and students can also monitor password resets by IT teams, so the wait time is minimal.

The application program interface (API) can quickly synchronize Google Classroom rosters with other systems, such as a learning management system or a student information system.

In the classroom area, API also allows teachers to use add-ons and other devices easily.

Google Classroom administrators have access to all types of data. You can monitor patterns of use, active users and classes, and posts made by students and teachers.

Teachers can provide input in real-time that is impossible in a pure pencil-and-paper environment. Google tools and software have built a networking atmosphere that allows even younger students in challenging circumstances to reach out to their teachers. Second-grade students in California's Arcadia Unified School District also contact their teachers when they have issues with their assignments.

CHAPTER 12:

Tips and Tricks

Communicate With Guardians

You may welcome guardians to pursue a regular or weekly email once-over on what's going on in classes for their youngsters. The messages contain pending or missed assignments for an student, and updates and questions that you have gotten in the class stream.

Help Students Remain Organized With Google Calendar

For every exercise, Classroom consequently produces a Google Calendar and updates the schedule with future research and due dates for the students. Students will see things; for example, study days and field trips. The schedule makes it simpler to keep on target. Since new assignments or changed due dates naturally synchronize, students, despite everything, see the most cutting-edge material.

Assign Work To A Subset Of Students

Instructors may designate individual students or a gathering of students inside a class to work and post declarations. This component causes instructors to isolate guidance varying, just as the care group works in a coordinated effort. To discover how these function, look at the image below.

Use Comments With The Classroom Portable Application

Students and instructors can utilize Classroom programming on cell phones running Android, iOS, or Chrome. By commenting on student exams in the app, you can give continuous criticism. Students may likewise comment on their assignments to pass on a thought or idea without much effort.

Use Private Comments for Reflection

A few instructors take the private remarks and make it part of the task by necessitating that students include a reflection as a private remark after they present their activity. Sean Fahey recommends utilizing an open-finished inquiry or give students a brief like, "What did you like most about the task?" or "What part tested you the most?"

Attach a Template Document for Each Assignment

You can see the Task page in Google Classroom, and see a thumbnail for every student. That permits you to see change initially or the absence of it.

Regardless of whether you have a format for your undertaking (that you include a spared dark report as a kind of perspective), you can at present get a brief look at the thumbnails!

Create a Demo Student Record To Show Google Classroom To Your Students

Right now, Google Classroom doesn't give educators an approach to see their classes as a student. Furthermore, you should have an student record to see your class as an student.

An answer proposed by Julie Sweeney Newton is to utilize an example record, and sign in as an student to perceive how the classroom functions and to show how to utilize the Classroom for your students. It is basic on the off chance that you approach manufacture Google Accounts in the area of your school.

That sort of access isn't available to most educators. For this situation, contact technical support to see whether a preliminary record can be obtained.

Package your Digital Assignments

This guide is a progression of tips to augment how students will require your headings, and group them into their Google Classroom assignments.

Engaging and Interactive Content

Consider exchanging the apparatuses you share with them in Google Classroom to make learning with computerized content progressively intelligent for students. Besides G Suite assets, for example Google Docs and Google Slides, instructors and students can share other media structures, including photographs, site joins, YouTube recordings, and screencasts. A few instructors have a scope of decisions for students to apply for their work inside Google Classroom as well.

The Stream is a feed inside Google Classroom where everybody in the class will discover fresh and forthcoming assignments. It is the principal thing students see when they sign in.

Learn All The Ways To Give Feedback

Your students will thrive with as much feedback as you can provide them, and Classroom offers you many options for this. You can leave comments on assignments that students hand in, on the file that is submitted, through email, and also do so much more. Consider the best places to leave feedback and let your students know so they can be on the lookout for ways to improve.

Use The Description Feature

When creating an assignment, make sure to add a nice long description. This is where you explain what the assignment is all about, how to complete it, and even when the assignment is due. Often students are juggling many classes all at once and by the time they get to the assignment, they have forgotten all the instructions you gave them in class. If a student missed class that day, the description can help them understand what they missed. A good description can help to limit emails with questions and can help students get started on the assignment without confusion.

Hidden Features of Google Classroom

Over the past years, Google Classroom has become a notable learning stage for certain, teachers using G Suite for Education. With its capacity to reliably fuse G Suite gadgets (Google Docs, Slides, Sheets, Gmail, and Calendar), Google Classroom makes a capable work process for instructors and students by organizing assignments and class content in an easy-to-investigate online condition. While Google Classroom gives various unfathomable benefits, three explicitly can save teachers and students a great deal of time and increase work process viability. Thus, we should use these energizing features!

The Assignment Calendar

Google Classroom makes an Assignment Calendar to help keep students and teachers updated. Each time a teacher makes an assignment or question in Google Classroom and interfaces a due date to it, the assignment immediately appears on the class plan inside Google Classroom.

The Work Area

Instructors and students can use the Work page inside Google Classroom to amass each extraordinary errand into one region. In case an educator has not assessed a particular errand, it will show at this moment.

Subsequently, if a student has not turned in an errand it will appear in their Work area. Along these lines, the work an area can fill in as a de facto task list and can bolster teachers and students to recognize and manage their work procedure satisfactorily.

How Google Classroom Can Help In Your Organization

There are also a lot of other great ways that you can use Google Classroom to makes your life a little bit easier. Some other things that you can consider doing with your Google Classroom Account include:

Google Forms

One of the features that you can do with Google Classroom is to use Google Forms. These make it really easy for the teacher to obtain information from their students, and for the students to leave some feedback about assignments, the class, and more. To keep this simple, the teacher can set up a Google Form to open up responses from people in the class. They can ask some open-ended questions, send out a survey, or something else. When the student is done with the survey, it will be marked as complete, so the teacher knows when the information is all complete.

Google Calendar

The Google Calendar is all automated on the system, so this makes it easier for students and teachers to keep track of the things that they need to work on when they are in a particular class. Whenever a teacher puts up a new assignment, project, test, or another thing for the students to work on, the due date is automatically going to be placed in and synced with the Google Calendar.

Use the About Page

One thing that a lot of students will forget to use is the **About** page because they don't think that it is all that important for them. But filling out this page can be really good for everyone involved. For the teacher, it is a good idea to fill in the **About** page with accurate information to help the student understand what class they are taking and who the teacher is. For example, the teacher may want to consider writing a good description of the particular class as well as give links to their website, a little bit about themselves, and their contact information, in case a student needs to get ahold of you.

Reuse The Posts

One of the nice things that a teacher will be able to do with Google Classroom is that they can take some posts that they used before, in another class or a previous class, and then reuse them a bit. This can be announcements, assignments, and even questions from their previous classes to help them keep up with the work, especially if the information still works with this current class.

Setting The Theme

Some students go into their Google Classroom and leave everything the way it is. They are happy with the theme and how everything is set up, so they don't want to switch anything around. But if you would like to personalize your Google Classroom, you can do that by changing some of the settings inside of Google Classroom. There are many different color palettes that you can choose from as well as different themes. You can experiment with this a little bit to find what works the best for your account.

In order to set up a new theme that you want to use in Classroom, you can use the following steps:

Open up Class

- From here, you can select the **Theme** button that is at the bottom of the image in your image settings.

- Now you can either select an image from the gallery or you can click on the **Patterns** button to pick out the theme that you would like.

- Once you have picked out what you would like to have there, you can click on **Apply** and the new theme is going to be all set up.

- It is also possible to upload some of your own pictures to the gallery in order to use that when picking out the new theme that you are using.

Find Conversation Starters

This is one that the teacher is most likely going to work with, but as a student, you will be able to go through and see what conversation starters the teacher has posted for you. You should be on the lookout for these to see what the teacher is asking for, such as feedback on the recent announcements, or even information about the discussion groups that you need to respond to for a grade.

This is a fantastic way for you to keep everyone in the class united, even if they are all in different locations.

Send Out Emails

Since this is a Google program, you will be able to use the Gmail account to send out emails to other people in the class. The teacher will be able to choose whether to send out an email to individual students if they need to, or they can pick out groups of students that they need to share information with, such as new announcements for the whole class.

Check Progress

While the student is working on the project, the teacher will be able to check how well the student is doing simply by clicking on the **Submission History**. They click on **Assignment Status** to check the history to see whether or not the student has been following the guidelines that were set for the assignment or if the work is just sitting there. It helps the teachers to keep track of who is getting the work done, and who may need a little bit of encouragement and can hold some students accountable.

Better Accessibility

Google Classroom can be accessed from any device that uses Google Chrome, regardless of platform. This means, you can work on your assignments on an iPad, or even on a mobile phone, and they're uploaded to Google Drive and the classroom folder, meaning they can be used wherever and whenever.

Students never have to worry about losing their assignments anymore, that's for sure!

Saves Paper!

Google Classroom is completely paperless, so you won't have to worry about printing thirty-plus copies for students who have a knack for losing their papers. You also do not have to worry about students misplacing paper because it's all online.

All of the assignments are uploaded there, and once there, they're saved to the Drive, which means that students can complete the assignments there, send it, and it's saved to Drive, and even if they don't save it, it's there so you never have to worry about students using the "my computer crashed" excuse for the third time.

Super Easy to Get Materials

It's also super easy to access the materials, but this is good because no matter where they end up, they'll get the materials. Absent students can get the classroom materials from home if needed by simply logging in and getting the assignments by clicking on this. Gone are the days of dealing with students having to chase after you just to get assignments.

All Work Is There

One thing that's super annoying and frustrating for teachers is the fact that some students have a knack for losing work. Well, Google Classroom nips that in the bud. How? Well, it takes out that external document, and instead, everyone works in Google Drive.

Google Drive saves everything immediately, regardless of if you make one change to add a word, or if you work on the assignment for hours on end. It's super nice, and it saves you a lot of headaches. It's all there, and students never have to worry about "accidentally" losing work.

Creates Collaborative Learning

Because everything is digital, you can share content with peers in one single document that can be edited together, and then share another version for the students without the editing to this. If you want to, you can create assignment worksheets that are different for teachers and students, and from there, Drive together with a question and answer system, and even create deeper discussions. It allows teachers to really engage with students.

With the way technology is bringing everyone together, it's no wonder why teachers want to integrate this further and further into the classroom.

Instant Feedback and Analysis

Gone are the days of waiting for whether did well on a quiz or whether you will get enough answers. Teachers don't have to sit around and meticulously spend a ton of time grading assignments. Instead, they can deliver quizzes that have automatic answers, or even give a detailed report on what teachers can do better. You can help those who answered questions incorrectly and add more to this, which is super nice. It is super easy to integrate into the system. Students will get their answers faster, and teachers can grade everything in a more detailed way.

Saves You a Ton of Time

For students, this saves them a ton of time trying to save various documents, hoping that it gets to their Drive, or even just working on paper and awkwardly turning it in. It also saves them time on answering questions, because let's be honest, a day could go by and they may not get the answer right away. By utilizing Google Classroom, you can save yourself a boatload of time, and ultimately participate way more as well.

Communication Success!

This ties into the point, but Google Classroom saves you a ton of time when it comes to communicating. If a student has a question, they can send an email, comment on an assignment stream, send comments privately, or even provide feedback on something. Teachers can do the same and can send specific emails to communicate with students that have a specific issue, or who need a lot more help. That way, they won't fall behind. It is making a difference in terms of how students handle the workload, and teachers can also follow the different standards. In truth, it makes it so much easier for everyone.

Students Take Ownership

One thing that teachers try to help students get better at, is trying to stay more engaged in their studies. Well, Google Classroom can help with this. It is not just students reading and commenting on answers that the other students may have; it is also being in charge of their homework. Students can teach a subject they're having trouble with a little bit better if they are struggling with it. In turn, if they want to utilize additional resources on their won, they can. The best part of Google Classroom is just that students can take charge of their learning environment, and in turn, create the best learning experience that they can.

Good Security

The security is actually very strong on this. If you have an IT team, they can control the passwords so if a student does forget, they can fix it quickly. With the API that is there, everything is synced, so the teachers can have everything put together. It's also got high-level security, which means that you won't have to worry about any breaches, etc., as it's also quite easy to work with.

See Real-Time Progress

Are you sick of trying to have to walk around and see whether students are working on this? Or maybe you want to help students if they are going in the wrong direction? Well, now you can address this. In Google Classroom, press Student Work to look at the thumbnail of every student to see their progress in real-time. You can track and see if there are any problems if you are looking to change this. You can also use the revision history feature to look at changes that have happened, allowing you to see what worked or what didn't work, and how you can fix that.

See All the Work

Finally, with a new update, you can look at the student's work. This is great if you know that a student is missing an assignment and they are claiming they turned it in. Teachers can do anything from making conferences to even meetings and study groups with Google classroom through the use of their system. You also look at all of the work that a student has put in, meticulously choosing different ways to help students benefit from their studies and other resources too.

CHAPTER 13

Advanced Options

Make Class Announcements

Teachers can publish statements to the Stream and send an email to the trainees' Gmail accounts. Students can locate older statements by scrolling down in the Stream. Google Classroom, likewise, permits trainees to make remarks on the statement.

Share Resources

Google Classroom permits instructors to take a file, link, or video and push it out to their students. Using Google Classroom, as the constant area for trainees to acquire digital resources, takes full advantage of class guideline time. Students are not being directed to several locations to find resources.

Keep Multiple Files in an Assignment

Google Classroom allows for several attachments to a single task. Teachers can appoint the students' multi-phase projects and offer a template for each of the different stages.

Develop a Lesson

The description area of the project allows the teacher to provide instructions to students for finishing the lesson and assignment.

Motivate Classroom Collaboration

When creating a project, the teacher can pick whether documents are shared as "View Only" or that files are shared so students can edit. By selecting **Students can modify the file**, all trainees in the class can edit the same document at the same time. This enables every student to contribute to a class project or activity.

Reduce Cheating

The task folder is available by the teacher only. Considering that the class files are not in a shared folder, the students cannot copy another trainees' work from the folder.

Produce a Discussion

A Google spreadsheet can be used to gather trainee concepts on a discussion topic. Conversation concerns can be included on a specific page, and extra tabs can be used for multiple concerns.

When trainees might have a hard time speaking up in class, this enables all trainees to have a voice in the discussion even.

The spreadsheet discussion likewise permits the trainees to view their schoolmates' concepts to compare and contrast the ideas with their own. Trainee actions can be dragged around the sheet to articulate patterns and distinctions in student viewpoints.

Organize Assignments with Due Dates

When creating a task in Google Classroom, the teacher can appoint a due date that is clear for both the teacher and the trainees. Google Classroom displays assignments that are not yet due on the Classroom tile for the trainee to see immediately after logging in.

Email Students

Sending an email to trainees is easy through Google Classroom. Educators can email trainees from any task page or go to the trainees' pages to send emails to selected private trainees or all trainees.

Email Feedback

Directly from Google Classroom, the instructor has two alternatives for emailing feedback to trainees. The first alternative is for the instructor to send a global note to the entire class.

The second option enables the teacher to send an email to an individual trainee.

Disperse Notes

Using a Google Doc in Google Classroom enables trainees to concentrate on class activities and conversations rather than note-taking. The teacher can publish the notes from the lesson in the class as an announcement.

Email the Teacher

Google Classroom gives students an icon to email the instructor. Clicking the icon launches a new message window. Because the e-mail will come from the trainee's GAFE account, the teacher can be sure the message is from that student.

File Digital Work

Teachers can create a task in Google Classroom and have trainees provide the link to their non-Google digital work. On the project submission page, the trainees have the alternative to a URL.

The students can attach websites, wikis, or other digital resources by linking to them in Google Classroom.

Trainees Create Google Docs

When viewing the project submission page, trainees can click **Create**, which permits them to begin a new Google Document, drawing, discussion, or spreadsheet. This file is immediately attached to Google Classroom and titled the same as the assignment.

The document title is added with the trainee name and saved in the assignment folder in Google Drive.

Clearly Identify Student Work

When a document is shared with trainees using the option **Each trainee gets a copy**, the new file shares the title of the design template file, and the student's name is added to the document title.

View Assignments

The instructor's list is split to show tasks "to review" and projects that are currently "reviewed." This makes it simple for the instructor to rate and assess student work. In the trainee view, students can find all the assignments that the teacher has published.

Offer Choices

Offering students options is not just a terrific method to separate direction; it also lets students have control in their learning. This leads to increased trainee engagement and inspiration. In the instructions of a Google Classroom assignment, the teacher can provide various choices for trainees to demonstrate finding out objectives. A recommendation is to label each choice with a name, such as

A, B, C, and so on. The teacher can then supply design templates for the various options in the assignment accessories.

Connect Directly to Student Work

When trainees send assignments, their files are offered through a link in Google Classroom. When instructors click on a submission, they are linked straight to the trainees' files without having to search for them in Google Drive.

Collect Data

The instructor can share a Google Form with trainees as an announcement in the Stream.

This permits trainees to arrange their information directly on the spreadsheet. Asking students to crowdsource resources onto a single document is another quick way to gather information from trainees.

Collaborative Notetaking

Collective notetaking is a great method for students to have a total set of class notes. The instructor can develop a Google document and share it as **Students can modify the file** in a project.

Then the instructor can designate specific students to be note-takers for a discussion or activity.

Show Student Work

When trainees send work in Google Classroom, their work is saved in a folder in Google Drive. The instructor can connect files by developing a brand-new statement and clicking the Google Drive alternative. With a student's consent, the teacher can share an announcement with a link to the student's work that is offered in his/her Classroom Google Drive folder.

Target Parent Phone Calls

Google Classroom reveals which trainees did not complete an assignment. By clicking the number above **NOT DONE**, the instructor is supplied with a list of students whose assignments have not been sent.

CHAPTER 14:

Most Common Online Teaching Challenges

Complex Account Management

Google Classroom doesn't enable multi-domain access. Also, you can't sign in to access your personal Gmail; you need to sign in to Google Apps for Education. As a consequence, if you already have your own Google ID, managing Google Accounts can be challenging. For example, if your Gmail contains a Google document or a picture and you want to share it in the Google Classroom, you need to save it separately on the hard drive of your device, log out, and then log in with your Google Classroom account again. It is much trouble.

Too 'Googlish'

Google users can get confused for the first time, as there are several buttons with icons that are only familiar to Google users.

Also, despite improved collaboration between Google and YouTube, of which the latter dramatically helps with video sharing, support for other standard tools is not built in. You can find it annoying that you need to convert a Word document to a Google Doc in order to work. All in all, in the Google Classroom environment, you'll only find yourself relaxed as long as the resources you're using fit with Google services.

Problems Editing

When you create an assignment and send it to the learners, the learners become the document's owners and are allowed to edit it. This means they can erase any part of the assignment they choose, which may create problems, even if unintentionally, it happens. Also, after you edit a post, students don't get a notification.

Isolation

No-one will hear you scream in an online course. This, for some online students, creates discomfort. It can be frightening to research alone with only the machine as your companion. There's no whispering in the back of the school, no wise peanut-gallery comments, no imposing voice at the front of the classroom, begging everyone to listen.

Own the Responsibility

It's just you who are responsible for knowing. No one can put that on you or get you to read. Teachers can only share some information and experience and give you a couple of tools, hoping you'll get it. You must have the spark and the drive to fulfill your dreams. So, the only downside of an internet-based course, in a rational way, is that you do not own it.

The Problem For Instructors

Online education is also a bit of a challenge for instructors. As tech progresses, teachers are continually trying to keep up. Traditional professors believe in lectures, so handouts and transition to the online course program can be difficult.

Technology Costs and Scheduling

The most critical elements of online courses are software programs and internet access. Students may need to learn new skills of programming and troubleshooting, which may take time. Students may also need to purchase new software to access their online classes or pay extra for upgrading to high-speed internet. Another drawback is that students need to change their schedules according to the due dates of assignments, which could be troublesome for international students or others who don't live in the same time zone as the teachers.

Communication Breakdowns

Often, you'll give your instructor an e-mail and wait for a reply. Three days pass, and you eventually get a response that is, at best, ambiguous.

So, you're e-mailing back, demanding clarity. Another three days pass, and you're getting another comment you don't quite understand. Quickly, a week has gone by, and you're still trapped in the dark. That is the truth for a lot of teachers and students who aren't updated with technology.

Group Work Can Be Challenging

Many university degrees nowadays impose group research as a prerequisite to passing the degree. The ability to work in teams is a preparation capability for the workplace that employer organizations believe is ingrained into a degree. When it comes to studying online, you are not other than needing to do group work.

Dreaded are the communities of students who study online. The fact that they're interacting with somebody they have never met physically scares them. So, they're reliant on their partners to log in continually. The trick with online community work is to try and locate a partner who will regularly and early in the week post on the forums. If you're working with one of those dedicated learners, you're going to do well.

Plagiarism and Cheating

Keeping in mind that students use a computer and are not always being monitored, they may plagiarize essays and other assignments. Along similar lines, cheating in online tests can be easier for students. Online cheating is easier to do (and more difficult to detect). Although it's not clear if online students are potentially cheating more than face-to-face students, the fact is that it's not easier to track who is taking a test and how they do it online compared to in a classroom.

CHAPTER 15:

FAQs About Google Classroom

A s a teacher, there are a lot of different options that you can use to make the most out of your classroom and you may be curious as to why Google Classroom is the best option to help you out. There are many questions that you may have that pertain to Google Classroom. Some of the questions that you may have about Google Classroom including the below.

Is it easy to get started with Google Classroom?

Yes, it is really easy to work with Google Classroom, but you do need to remember that it is necessary to have the Google Apps for Education and your domain needs to be verified.

How are the apps for education and classroom connected?

To keep things simple, Google Classroom is not able to work without the help of Google Apps for Education. While you can use the Apps for Education all on its own, you will find that using Google Classroom is going to help to make all of it organized, and it is much easier to work with. With the help of both the Classroom and apps working together, both the students and the teachers can access the spreadsheets, slideshows, and documents as well as other links without having to worry about attachments, etc.

Even giving and receiving assignments and grades are easier when these two are combined together.

Does it cost to use Google Classroom?

One of the best things about using Google Classroom is that it is completely free. All you need is a bit of time to help get it all set up, but it will not include any out-of-pocket costs to make it work.

You will have to wait about two weeks in the beginning for your application to be reviewed before you can use the class, so consider setting this up early to prevent issues with falling behind.

You will never have to pay for anything when you are using Google Classroom. If you run into a vendor who is asking for you to pay for Google Classroom, you should report them to Google.

It is highly likely that this is a fake vendor so do not work with them or provide them with any of your payment information. Google Classroom is, and always will be, free for you to use.

Can I still use Classroom if it is disabled on my domain?

One of the nice things about working with Classroom is that even if it has been disabled on a certain domain, you are still able to use it. With that being said, there are going to be a few restrictions. While you may still be able to get access to a lot of the features, such as Google Drive, Google Docs, and Gmail, you may not be able to see some of the slides, docs, and sheets that were saved in the classroom. It is always best to have your domain turned on when you are working in Google Classroom because this ensures that you can use all of the features that are available through the Classroom.

Do I need to have Gmail enabled to use Classroom?

It is not necessary to have Gmail enabled in order to use the Google Classroom. You can use the Classroom as much as you would like without enabling Gmail, but you would find that you wouldn't be able to receive notifications if the Gmail account isn't turned on. If you would like to have some notifications sent to you, you need to have Gmail enabled.

If you are not that fond of using the Gmail account for this, it is possible to set up your own email server to make it work.

This way, you will still be able to receive the notifications that are needed from the Classroom while using the email server that you like the most.

Will I have to work with ads on Google Classroom?

Many people like to work with Google Classroom because they don't have to worry about seeing ads all over the place. Classroom was designed for educational purposes, and Google recognizes that people shouldn't have to fight with ads all of the time when they are learning. You can rest assured that Google and Classroom are not going to take your information and use it for advertising. This is part of the privacy and security that is offered with Google Classroom, which will protect both the student and the teacher from any phishing or spam.

If I have a disability, am I able to use Google Classroom?

Yes, those with disabilities can use Google Classroom. Some of the features are not yet complete, but Google is working to make some improvements to Classroom so that those who have disabilities can use it too. Aside from using the Screen reader, there are a few other features that you can use with Android.

You can also tweak some of the settings that are in Google Classroom regarding color correction, magnification, captions, touch and hold, using a speaking password, and more.

As you can see, there are a lot of neat things that you can do when it comes to using Google Classroom and it is pretty easy for everyone to be able to use. If you ever have some other questions about Google Classroom, you can always contact their support to get the assistance that you need.

Conclusion

So, you have read this book and have gained some concepts about using Google Classroom. Congratulations on taking strides to enhance your students' education and experiences in your classroom! Comprehending brand-new innovation and its capabilities is an exceptional place to begin. We have to caution you though: only using Google Classroom to disperse and gather worksheets will not enhance your classroom or engage your students.

Just using Google Classroom will not have a considerable change in your teaching. If your class is teacher-focused, it will not matter what tools and technology you use; you'll get the same results in any case.

However, when you combine the approaches we've shared with strong, student-centered pedagogy and effective educational methods, your trainees can participate more and will be delighted about the learning process.

We have shown you how Google Classroom can assist you to do a lot more: linking students with resources, developing engaging and motivating guidelines, and creating your classroom as a partnership.

This book consists of only fifty ideas for using Google Classroom, but there are numerous more ways this resource is being used.

Above all, never let your teaching end up being static or ordinary. Continue to explore ways to improve and sharpen your mentoring skills.

As the saying goes, "School's never out for the pro."

Learning is something that can be made fun, and with Google Classroom, you can achieve that and so much more.

Your next step is to work with Google Classroom. Play around with it and make it so that you know how to use the system, whether you're a teacher, student, or parent.

Through understanding what you're using, you can create a conducive learning environment that works for everyone. Teachers will soon notice that students are better with this (they'll be more involved) and parents can keep an eye on anything that's going wrong, which creates a better classroom, and a more beneficial learning experience for everyone, and it does change the game by a lot as well for everyone.

Good luck.

AN EASY PROFESSIONAL STEP-BY-STEP GUIDE
TO QUICKLY LEARN HOW TO RUN BUSINESS
MEETING AND WEBINARS FOR YOUR WORK OR
TEACHING ACTIVITIES FOR YOUR CLASSROOM

MARY B.
FREEMAN

ZOOM FOR
BEGINNERS

Introduction

Z oom is a cloud-based video conferencing service that you can use to meet others by video, audio, or both while making live chats, allowing you to view the sessions and lets you record them.

Zoom meetings are virtual video conferencing meetings that are hosted using Zoom. You can join meetings through a webcam or phone.

Zoom Rooms are physical setups companies or people use to schedule Zoom meetings from their conference rooms.

Zoom rooms need an additional subscription and is suitable for large companies.

Zoom was launched in 2011 but has recently garnered a lot of attention due to the COVID-19 pandemic. Whether it is for online classes, business meetings, informal gatherings, or group practices, Zoom seems to be the number-one tool for staying connected to the outside world amidst this gloomy quarantine. And, with numerous entertaining and unique features, it is highly preferred when compared to the other video conferencing services.

Since its launch, Zoom has actually been trending in Europe and the United States and also across the world. Unlike other video conferencing services that allow no more than 4 to 5 people to share a screen at one time, Zoom allows hundreds of participants at a time (based on your subscription plan).

But, with so many other video conferencing services available, what is the appeal of Zoom, and what has led people to use this platform more than other services?

Apart from its exciting features, it all boils down to its reliability and accessibility.

Currently, the world is facing a morbid pandemic, and most people are advised to stay at home to prevent COVID-19 from spreading further. This horrific situation has not only ruined normal business operations but has also impacted our social lives. Large-scale conferences and events, such as Milan Design Week, Google's Annual Developer's Conference, the tech and music festival, SXSW, major sports events like Formula 1, and even the Olympics 2020, have been canceled this year to avoid public gatherings and respect the norms of social distancing.

In this situation, people are trying to conduct business, conferences, and necessary meetings through video calls. A few months ago, video conferencing services were mere conveniences or added benefits to any work environment. Now, with the obligation of social distancing, these have quickly become a necessity. Employees have to work from home, and video calls are one of the ways to stay connected with your boss, colleagues, clients, or students (if you are a teacher). Students are duty-bound to learn online, through lessons that are conducted over video conferences. Because of this, teachers, businessmen, lawyers, and most employees in general, are trying to learn this new technology.

Here enters Zoom. This name was barely known across the world before COVID-19 struck and people were pushed to stay at home. Almost every business, school, university, and the informal party started using Zoom, which led to a massive surge in its popularity, so much so, that the company noted 2.2 million new users every month over the past few months (since lockdown measures were established). Its overnight success made it a popular name in every household. It's almost a given that you have heard the name a few times during this lockdown.

If you aren't entirely familiar with it, let us break it down for you. Zoom is a video conferencing platform that allows multiple users to access relevant video conference meetings at the same time. Whether it is your office meeting or a virtual gathering with your long-distance family, Zoom can keep you connected at all times.

In the past, Zoom was only restricted to big corporations, businesses with large teams, or companies that worked with virtual assistants or digital nomads. With the recent practice of social distancing, most companies and clients are switching to Zoom to stay connected and keep the work flowing. While companies that require a physical presence have suffered tremendously, video conferences have greatly aided the companies that can work virtually.

It is one of the first video and audio-conferencing software that is available in personal computer and smartphone variants. The user experience is top-notch, which has come in handy in the time of social distancing. Below are things you require:

- An online computer, laptop, smartphone, or tablet (find the app in the Apple Store or Play Store)

- Headphones/Air pods/earphones

- Call phone (optional) and microphone or webcam microphone

- After downloading the Zoom program to your computer or smartphone, you can use the user card to work in the Zoom connector.

- The Home tab contains all the basics of the meeting: Start with a video, Start without a video, Connect, Schedule, and Share on-screen.

CHAPTER 1:

Communicating and Collaborating In Zoom

C ommunication is an essential part of any success-driven organization, and as such, video conferencing is inevitable. Video conferencing applications, like Zoom, enable individuals to meet and work together gainfully without having to meet physically.

Excellent communication is all about making things easier, and who wants to travel to a meeting for hours?

Eighty-nine percent of remote teams use video conferencing to communicate with colleagues or managers, according to a new survey. The same study explains that about 75% of U.S. corporate workers use video communication to work remotely, with a majority showing higher productivity and a stronger work-life balance.

You can say goodbye to Monday's rush hour, corporate attire, and mundane office environments, thanks to communication apps like Zoom. The software for video conferencing allows you to go to work without the need to leave the comfort of your home. It's a response to the latest working-style trend —

remote working. Wherever you are, Zoom will ensure all stakeholders can remain on track and work successfully together.

The remote conferencing platform uses cloud computing to invite users to hold online meetings and conferences. It also includes instant messaging, screen sharing, **etc.** This software offers four different plans that suit your needs best, making it a popular professional online tool.

While many businesses are already using the Zoom video conferencing app for business meetings, interviews, and other purposes, individuals facing long days without contacting friends and family are moving to Zoom for face-to-face and group get-togethers.

The Zoom platform is an American innovation created by Eric Yuan, who is a former executive and Webex engineer. He founded the platform in the year 2011 and introduced software for the platform in the year 2013. It offers chat services online and video-telephony via peer-to-peer software, based on the cloud. Users can utilize it to perform several tasks like social relations, video calls, and communications, teleconferencing, and lots more. It is a straightforward platform with different types of exceptional attributes that are essential for remote workers. These workers can utilize the platform for their productivity enhancement. The platform has a strategy for the business that focuses on offering an alternative route for users to utilize an item more than the competitors. It also reduces costs, increases savings, and minimizes infrastructure costs.

It has excellent compatibility with Linux, Android, Windows, and the likes. The interface of the platform differs on each platform, and that depends on the type of device you utilize, which could be mobile or desktop. You can also utilize the platform to host meetings or connect with co-workers and employees. You can also create a connection between family and friends, and do lots more.

In the face of the present downturn in both personal and business environments, the Zoom app is now the new standard for getting in touch with others online in a face-to-face manner. Zoom is currently the social video interaction platform for businesses, tech startups, religious communities, and everyday people willing to talk with their family, friends, business partners, clients, specific homogenous groups, and even the governments of nations.

CHAPTER 2:

Webinar

Zoom Video Webinar enables you to transmit up to ten thousand view-only participants of a Zoom conference, based on the extent of your webinar permit. Webinar licenses begin at a capacity of a hundred participants and have a scale of up to ten thousand. You can display your computer, photo, and audio as the host or panel member in a webinar, and guests may use the talk or Q&A tools to connect with the moderator and panel members.

Pre-registration for Webinars

Webinars may involve pre-registration corresponding to the meeting. The host may either accept all registrants immediately or authorize them manually. The host will add queries regarding personalized registration and remove the registration files. Optionally, the webinar access may be switched off by the server. After entering, the passengers would also be asked to type their name, and email address, and the records should be restricted to this.

Registration Approval Methods

There are two webinar acceptance forms included in registration.

Approve Immediately: All webinar account holders should instantly obtain a confirmation email containing information about how to access the webinar.

Manually Accept: The Webinar host must manually authorize or deny the consent of a registrant. If a registered owner is accepted, an email with instructions about how to access the webinar will be sent to them.

Schedule Webinar

Log in to the online server for the Zoom. Select Webinars. The collection of planned webinars can be found here.

Choose a Webinar to Plan.

Use the webinar settings you need. Choose the date, time zone, topic, webinar password, and other registration settings.

Click to schedule a webinar.

Sending Invites

There are three ways to invite participants to sign up:

Copy and distribute the login URL via email address, websites, etc.

Click **Download the invitation** to show and send the email or link. Zoom has generated it to hand out to the participants.

Use email to ask to obtain a copy of the invitation to Zoom, which you will then forward to future attendees.

Sending Invitations to Join a Meeting or Webinar

There are many options to invite the members to an immediate or planned conference. You can also invite a space network (requires Web Space) by smartphone (allows the audio meeting plan).

Sending Invitations through URL

The conference members should only provide the URL of the group. The meeting URL is underscored in yellow in this case. Share this URL with your guests, and to continue the conference, they must click on it.

Whether you use web or smartphone devices, click on the Meetings page.

If you click on the **Copy Invitation** button on the mobile device. A notification with the address, name, and telephone dial-in details of your Zoom meeting will be copied to your clipboard, which you can drop in an email or text message.

Sending Invitations through Email

Once you click the **Send Invitation** button on the device, two choices will be given to you: **Send Email**, which will allow you to send your conference URL to someone; and **Copy to Clipboard**, which will transfer the URL of your Zoom meeting to the clipboard on your device.

Sending Invitations in Chats

Click on the icon in the **Participants** button on the mobile device on the menu that appears as you push your cursor in the Meeting tab, and then click on **Invite**.

If you do, Zoom will open a new window in which you can invite your Zoom contacts, submit a message with instructions about how to reach your Zoom group, copy your group URL to your clipboard or chats, or copy a longer message with your Meeting. You will also include code of your conference in this section.

Contacts

1. Tap on the Digital Contacts page.

2. From the window, pick their name or locate the email.

3. Tap on the user you want to invite. You can have several connections. When you do so, your name will be outlined in blue, which will display at the top of the screen in the column.

4. Select **Invite** button in the bottom-right corner.

Pros of Webinars

Easy Setup

The platform is easy to use, and you can easily download, click, and set it up.

It is the easiest video conferencing solution and the best innovation that happened recently in the business world. It functions almost with just a click and can connect to meetings easily as well as help users hold interactions with customers.

Minimize The Cost Of Traveling

The idea of traveling to meet people can drain your time and money. Zoom provide solutions to its users and the business world at large.

The introduction of video conferencing makes holding and managing meetings with participants easy within a few minutes from several remote locations across the world.

Binds Remote Employees

You can have workers all scattered in the various locations in the country or cities around you. The platform gives users the ability to connect workers. All of the workers can connect by use of smartphones.

Virtual Backgrounds

The platform lets users replace the space with their favorite pictures. It is an attribute that you can utilize across all devices besides Android, because it does not have high hardware demands. However, you can utilize the virtual background alternative, although the performance will differ.

Cons

Expensive

Utilizing the Zoom platform incurs additional costs because the platform comes with add-ons. You can remove that option in the basic plan level, which will make it less expensive. When you begin the addition of the extras, the price continues to go up with every inclusion.

Different Plan Patterns

The different platform plans are a benefit, but when it can become too much and you may hardly know which one to pick. You might even think of customizing your plan. The platform comes with different issues for different plans and can, in turn, send customers, who just want a basic plan to enjoy their services, away.

Slow Customer Services

Whenever you contact them, a representative can take about two to three days to give replies about solutions to a problem and how to fix them. It can be very frustrating and can put your business at risk.

It is really hard to find an organization, business or sector without the utilization of the Zoom platform to conduct their online meetings and video interactions among employees so you can understand why they have service delay problems.

Intrusion

The Zoom platform has a high vulnerability to cyber-attacks and hackers. Black hats can forcefully get passwords and take control over virtual and online meetings as well as post demeaning or offensive content to destabilize business activities.

CHAPTER 3:

Meetings

Starting a Meeting

1. Go on website *zoom.us*.
2. Switch over the line to "Hold a Conference" in the top-right corner.
3. Select whether you like video messaging switched on.
4. Sign in with your login details or create a new account.
5. Open the Zoom app, and access it.
6. Submit information about the meeting, including the Conference Identification Number and connection.
7. You generated a meeting!

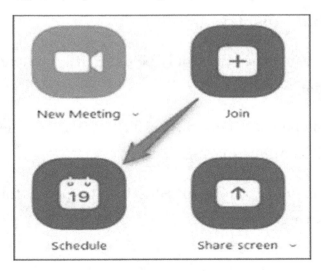

Audio Settings

When you are already in a conference, you can control your audio settings and check your performance.

1. Click the button next to **Mute/Unmute** in the controls of the conference.

2. Select **Options to Sound**. It will unlock your settings for audio.

3. To check the microphone or speaker, select the settings, and play a tutorial video.

Screen Sharing

1. Zoom lets users view the whole conference call with their phone or laptop!

2. To do so quickly click at the bottom of the window on **Share Display**.

3. Screen-sharing can only be done with one person at a time.

4. One person ought to **Avoid Sharing** so someone else will continue sharing.

5. Only click on **Stop Sharing** to pause the screen sharing.

Scheduling a Meeting

1. Enable your device with the Zoom application.

2. Tap on **Home** in the upper-left corner.

3. Select **Schedule a Meeting**.

4. Enter all related information such as period, place, topic, etc.

5. Choose your favorite online calendar (Internet Calendar is perfect if you have got Gmail or a Twitter account), and you will be brought to a page with your Zoom button. You may give the connection to your students in the meeting scheduler of your calendar.

Choose a Topic for your Meeting

While scheduling a Zoom meeting, you will be asked to add a suitable topic for your meeting so that people can see on what subject they are going to join the meeting. You can select any topic base on your preferences.

Choose a Time Zone

After selecting a topic, Zoom will ask you to choose a time zone. Choose your country to choose the time zone and pick an hour to schedule your meeting. Zoom will remind you through email when your meeting time will start.

Video and Audio Settings

When you are a host of the meeting, Zoom will ask you to manage your audio and video settings and controlling your meeting participant's video and audio settings. Basic options are about the microphone On/Off option and video On/Off option provided to your meeting participants.

Other Meeting Options

Other meeting options include setting an ID and password for your meeting and setting up a calendar. You can select **Require Meeting ID** or **Use Personal Meeting ID**. There is another option of enabling participants to enter before the host comes to the meeting. Based on your preferences, you can choose an option from that.

Joining a Meeting

1. Switch to *zoom.us*.

2. Click the **Click to Attend** button. You will locate the button at the upper right-hand side of the front screen corner.

3. Attach your assigned Meeting Identification when asked (the Meeting Identification may be a nine-, ten-, or eleven-digit number). The Conference identification will be given by the host.

4. You are inside!

Privacy and security

Zoom has a lot of features that can ensure that your meetings are private and well secured. The setup in your office might affect your security preferences but you can use your remote working setup to make your experience better. With Zoom, these are some of the things you can do to ensure better privacy:

You can allow only those who have the password to the meeting to join by locking the meeting.

You can admit users only when you are ready for them to join by using the Waiting Room feature.

You can restrict the participants in the meeting to only attendees with the same domain.

If your meeting content is sensitive, you can enable a watermark on audio and video in the background.

You can limit screen sharing to only content from the interface of a particular application rather than participants seeing the entire desktop. This can prevent participants from mistakenly seeing stuff on your desktop that they shouldn't.

CHAPTER 4:

Zoom on Phone

Zoom on Phone is a simple cloud-calling solution constructed for users that wish to install calls. You would turn into Zoom if you do not require the meetings; you can start a VoIP phone that is fast using the tools you already know and enjoy. Zoom turns complete with messaging, voice, messaging, and video at precisely the same solution.

The Benefits Of Zoom Phone

Perhaps Zoom Phone's biggest benefit is its ease of use. The application is intended to be as available as the remainder of the Zoom encounter, and therefore you don't have to download some applications that were intricate to utilize it.

From video to voice calls effortlessly, you can transition using Zoom Phone.

Rewards include:

- **The simplicity of use for everybody:** After you click on your Zoom customer, your telephone function will just appear alongside your Chat and Assembly choices. Click on your telephone, enter the contact number or an individual's name, and you are all set to go. It is simple.

- **Connect to outside platforms:** You can join your SIP alternative to outside programs from Five9 and Twilio too. In this manner, it is easier to handle your phone routing choices through a number of the world's favorite cloud phone providers.

- **BYOC:** Zoom is dedicated to innovating as promptly as possible for their clients so they can deliver performance that suits the whole Zoom expertise. The Bring Your Own Carrier (BYOC) alternative ensures you can access all of the benefits of Zoom Phone via your existing PSTN trunks.

- **Centralized Communication Management:** Zoom Telephone matches seamlessly with any consumer's digital transformation approach. The system enables companies and business leaders to manage and supply users publicly, track company interactions, and do much more in an easy admin gateway.

Target Market & Regional Availability

Zoom Phone is a great solution for any business that needs and adores the Zoom expertise, freedom calls, and meetings. The telephone system enables workers to socialize on a program they are knowledgeable about. Australian beta support and the UK for Zoom Phone became accessible per petition on the 19th of May. Zoom will roll out the service to markets in the foreseeable future.

Zoom Differs in Your Telephone, So Here Is The Way To Use It

During the coronavirus pandemic, video calls have been the newest way to run businesses and interact with friends and family members. Last week, by way of example, I played a digital game of trivia with over 130 participants from all over the globe; listened in on a job interview with 12 other people; had a household check-up together with my cousins and sister, who appreciated the a DJ Livestream—all through Zoom. For pursuits that are distinct, devices work. However, not everything works on the cellphone or program on an iPad as it does on your laptop. Different devices have different capacities, as Zoom describes on its site in addition to its own Google Play and Apple App shops. Although the company does not say it specifically, the Zoom expertise in your phone or tablet computer isn't quite as powerful as the version for Mac or Windows. Just examine screen sharing or the chat attributes on a cellular level. But that does not mean the program does not work for certain scenarios. Take Siri as an example. You can program the helper during the program. She cannot help you when your Mac gets Siri. There are reasons you may want to open your game up even though it seems like work.

View Manner

Notebook for Large Groups, Cellular for Romantic Chats

Anecdotally, it appears Zoom's mobile program is not too popular for work meetings because many men and women want the entire display to see graphs, files, and all their colleagues from the assembly. If your requirements are more productivity-focused, stick with a notebook for Zoom. The screen options that are limited to others are shown. On Zoom on your cellphone, you may have four faces displayed at one time correctly, but in your notebook, it is similar to credits opening. Gallery perspective lets up to 25 participants on a display since the Zoom website explains.

Chatting

Get Zoom Background to get a smoother experience. The Zoom conversation is its own thing. You can message everybody on a telephone or only message a player. It is refreshingly retro in its simplicity. The dialog slots on the side of this display or whether you are in Fullscreen mode becomes a floating window. However, when you begin using the conversation on cellular, it isn't quite as simple to use, or perhaps find. Clicking on the **More** button at the bottom of the program brings a conversation alternative, that then brings up a window which takes over the whole telephone and... it just gets messy. With the Zoom background experience, stick to side effects.

Screensharing

Mobile Program in A Pinch, Notebook for Anything Significant You can present your display by telephone, but it is not as easy as a procedure in a notebook. If you are introducing a slideshow or active display, your notebook will be simpler to share. It may get bizarre sharing your telephone display. Do it in case you've got a telephone.

Multitasking

More Difficult to Pull On Cell Phones

Let us be real here: you are not committed to just your Zoom call. If you are not introducing or leading a meeting, it is simple enough to look as if you are paying attention when doing anything else on your notebook. In your telephone, however, it is little more than a hassle to browse your email inbox.

Video

Mobile for On-The-Go Video

One of my co-workers uses the Zoom program on his mobile phone, especially because of its video purpose. He utilizes a rack so that the phone is an outside camera beside his PC. Then there are the seconds you might want to maneuver around through a Zoom telephone number. You are less likely nowadays to be commuting in the car (although you might be on the road to the supermarket). Only because you are trapped in your home does not mean that you want to be tethered to a notebook or the portion of your home designated as "the office." The cellular program provides you with freedom to move around, do some home chores, or look after a youthful co-worker.

Backgrounds

Seamless on Both the iPhone And Notebooks

You can alter your background on the iOS and variations, thank goodness. As entertaining as it is, it is not for Android consumers, sorry! However, so long as you've got an iPhone version 8 or above, you are set for cellular. Your desktop game can go large in case you've got a laptop. For computers, it can't probably be handled by the operating system. This may help you keep it professional.

In the autumn of 2018, Zoom declared its intent to round out its product package to incorporate every company communication utilize case, such as cross-platform workflows cloud PBX and business conference rooms. This was the arrival of Zoom cloud mobile system. Zoom introduced Zoom Phone in the first quarter of 2019 to North American clients (like Puerto Rico) and then to intended to extend into five additional nations (Canada, UK, Australia, Ireland, and New Zealand). Nowadays, Zoom phone calls have become as ordinary as Zoom video conferences. The continued attempts at Zoom increased the profile of Zoom cloud mobile system. Now, a bit over one year from the roll-out of Zoom Phone, the discussion centers around whether Zoom Phone can be prepared. This post gives a solution to this question.

Zoom Phone in Year 2

Zoom Phone was created to provide a unified communications supply and experience to Zoom clients. Just six months after, Gartner declared that from 2023, 40 percent of new venture telecom buys, will be contingent on a cloud Office package -- Microsoft Office 365. Zoom Phone has evolved into a strong cloud PBX that Zoom expects each client will embrace. Since the launch of Zoom Phone, Zoom has more than 200 features, certified over 50 phone models for its support, and started a beta application from Austria, Belgium, Denmark, France, Germany, Italy, Netherlands, Portugal, Spain, Sweden, and Switzerland. In case you've stumbled upon our site for the very first time, and are not certain what we do, then enable us to present ourselves and also to welcome you to **Unify Square**. Our services & software optimize and improve the world's biggest Microsoft Teams, Zoom, Skype, and company deployments. We're on a mission to empower adventures for conversations, meetings, and forecasts.

CHAPTER 5:

Advantage and Disadvantages

Advantages

The quality of the video is a significant device for employees who telecommute. In the event that you have a plan for your business and employees who telecommute, you can dispense an absence of correspondence in the gathering by video conferencing.

Meeting Association Early

Clients can perform gatherings without bobbling different applications for various reasons. It offers sound and video methods of correspondence just as sharing screens. Despite the fact that holding a gathering on the web is free and it assists clients in limiting costs and maintaining a strategic distance from limitations, clients can have gatherings unbounded. It gives distinctive businesses the necessary speed and encourages them to develop as the world moves forward.

Clients likewise can give short notifications on gatherings before it begins, and each chaperon will have no reason to travel or change the area. The main thing they have to do is give themselves the necessary opportunity. You can make a calendar for video gatherings in a single moment and guarantee that it runs the right way. It is an ideal preferred position for clients on a tight calendar.

Acculturate Associations

It can refine interchanges between chaperons or discussions between representatives. You should comprehend that a video is an assortment of moving pictures that can be worth more than one million words. The way toward indicating your face on the screen and taking a look at different specialists permits the presentation of non-verbal communication charms, which is a small leeway for entrepreneurs. Taking a look at an individual while holding a discussion with them gives a positive sentiment and changes the idea of the association, it doesn't make a difference if it is an individual relationship or a business one.

Things Show

It is a bit of leeway for business and association who wants to persuade their clients. At the point when they see the item live, it helps their certainty and makes trust just as persuade the client.

With the use of the video quality for conferencing, you can play out the assignment of composing on board and show it so everybody can see it.

Show the latest and most recent things that you need to sell or make a presentation of enlisted people, who will enable your business to develop. The stage allows clients to show things that they can't place in a bag or pass on, starting with one area, then onto the next, for gatherings on the video stage.

Web Instruction

There are various amazing courses that you will discover on the web and educators that are prepared to instruct; yet separation can turn into an issue. In the event that you are a coach or mentor that stays at a significant distance from your understudies, using Zoom makes the procedure direct. It is a brilliant idea of acquiring and circulating information without confronting any issues. In spite of the fact that you may not be available truly, that won't influence the assignment since it offers fantastic correspondence quality. You can use interactive media apparatuses, for example, community whiteboards and other aggregate instruments. Another significant advantage of Zoom is that regardless of the quantity of video calls, it doesn't lessen in quality, talks, and keeps on creating noteworthy sounds.

Secret Key Problems

Heaps of individuals overlook their secret key and ID routinely, yet the stage offers an answer. You needn't bother with the necessity of a login ID or pass-key, to use the stage or stress over overlooking your subtleties in light of the fact that with not many snaps you are up going for it. It likewise annihilates voice gabbing and guarantees that the individual on the opposite side can hear whatever you state to them, and the other way around. It is a clear and advantageous stage to utilize.

Astounding Sound and Video Administration

Checking the sound/video sounds and quality is an incredible method to know which stage gives the best administration. The Zoom stage is the head of that classification. The administration that the stage offers stands apart from its companions and gives fantastic video administration.

Its quality doesn't decrease even in pained areas that have low data transfer capacity or reverberation issues inside its gateways. It offers brilliant execution and doesn't experience any sort of issues while being used in any event, when the gathering specialists begin joining the rooms.

Online Gatherings

Another extraordinary nature of the stage is the irrefutable nature of its sound and video administrations for a few exercises.

The stage enables clients to create a URL and ID for the gathering and offer it with each chaperon. Be that as it may, clients must watch out for the utilization of the focal handling unit assets of the PC.

For instance, during a video meeting, the preparing unit can arrive at 100%, which can be a drawback since it will hinder the framework and influence its exhibition. On the off chance that you use the last forms of PCs, or if nothing else in two years, you may not confront any issues with your preparing unit, since it can oversee HD designs effortlessly and you play out your undertaking blunder free.

Versatility

You should comprehend that the Zoom stage is expandable. It is a dynamic arrangement, and dissimilar to different stages, it extends with an association to deal with the developing prerequisites. The capacity to grow enables organizations and entrepreneurs to change their abilities of cooperation to sum their representatives relying upon their necessities and size.

Flexibility

The stage guarantees that clients appreciate a brilliant encounter over each device, in light of its simple flexibility. It enables organizations and business associations to deal with each type of collaboration.

It doesn't make a difference that it is on a cell phone or work area. It helps employees, directors, and clients make a coordinated effort and place the utilization of the stage, regardless of whether it is in a vehicle, office, or home.

Valuing

The Zoom stage is moderate and has an extraordinary value structure for your business level and type. The valuing is an incredible apparatus for organizations and organizations that need to propel their collaborative approach with little ventures monetarily. It accompanies four distinct plans, with costs dependent on the number of hosts and the qualities they have.

The plans incorporate fundamental, business, expert, and undertaking. You will get a decent incentive for your speculation plan on the rudiments, and it is additionally an ideal decision for preparing the internet, sharing the screen, having official gatherings, and recording meetings. The free form offers just forty minutes for each gathering, and it keeps every meeting short.

Lessens Instruction Cost

The video property for instructive purposes spares a great deal of cost of fundamental hardware for the procedure. Many establishments and schools in distant territories don't have the necessary assets to create or broaden instructive structures for different reasons. Using the component is a brilliant choice for training in such territories. It likewise gives the understudies another perspective on the world, just like constructing another world for your students to see and learn things that they can't learn in an ordinary class.

Improves Mentor to Guardian's Association

Many mentors have any expectations of keeping close contact with guardians, which the stage made simple with the video quality that the two players can use to arrive at each other. The idea of video gatherings diminishes false imclick onions among guardians and educators. Presently guides don't have to welcome the parent-to-class gatherings anymore. They would now be able to use the stage to play out that task. Guardians can generally join the video meeting from the guide from any area on the planet with a web association.

Magnificent Help Arrangement on Moderate Systems

The stage offers awesome administrations across contraptions with moderate systems and can deal with any event and one hundred chaperons simultaneously. It gives a decent domain to online courses and business gatherings. The times of transfer speed issues are over on the grounds that your information has a cloud worker back up. You should realize that a limit of one hundred specialists can share the screen and execute significant communication from a far-off zone.

It Gives A Bound-Together Stage

Specialists can connect with each other at whatever point they need with the use of live visits during cooperation. It doesn't have a limitation on virtual/online gatherings and online courses.

Along these lines, whenever you need to convey or share information or pose inquiries, you can play out that task with the live talk highlight.

Disadvantages

The extension of administrations to the training and the business social insurance division guarantees that the Zoom stage arrives at its possible pinnacle.

In spite of the fact that the stage is the best for your business necessities, it additionally has its confinements, which can be a weakness to its clients.

Heaps of scientists have discovered a few burdens of the stage, which incorporates encroachment of security strategy and the preferences.

The following pages describe cons of using the Zoom stage.

<u>Costly</u>

Using the Zoom stage brings about extra expenses on the grounds that the stage accompanies additional items. You can expel that choice on the essential arrangement level, which will make it more affordable.

At the point when you start the expansion of the additional items, the value keeps on going up with each consideration.

Diverse Arrangement Designs

The diverse stage sorts of plans are an advantage. However, it turns out to be excessive and you scarcely know which one to pick. You may even consider modifying your arrangement. The stage accompanies various sorts of issues for various plans and can, thus, send clients who simply need a fundamental intend to take most of their administrations away.

Slow Client Administrations

An agent can take around a few days to give answers to an issue and how to fix it when you reach them. It tends to be exceptionally disappointing and can put your business in danger.

It is an extremely elusive association, business, or part without the use of the Zoom stage to lead their online gatherings and video communications among workers, so you can comprehend why they have administration delay issues.

CHAPTER 6:

Tips and Tricks

Even though we all know that you are likely to be at home when participating in a Zoom meeting, it's still important to note that one should try to look presentable especially if the meeting is a formal or work meeting. So, I'm going to share my top tips and tricks for looking your best in Zoom meetings.

1. Use the Most Suitable Lighting

Generally speaking, the best lighting is going to be diffused natural light from a window that you're sitting directly in front of. Any light that's coming from above you or from the side or from the back is not going to be that flattering because it's going to cast shadows or it's going to backlight you. However, if you're going to sit by a window, make sure that you're not going to sit in front of a window that gives you full exposure to direct sunlight because the lighting will just be too bright, and it will blast you.

Before a video Zoom meeting, try to find out the area of the room or house that has the best lighting angle, so you won't be embarrassed trying to adjust your position when the meeting starts. You can do this by using your phone camera to walk around the house or room to get the best angle.

To further enhance the lighting of your video, you can bring the bed lamp close to you or even put just opposite your face so that the light is shining directly on your face. You can also get a ring light if you can get access to it.

2. Use Your Most Suitable Camera Angle

Just like we were looking for the most flattering light, you've also got to be looking for the most flattering camera angle. I found out that the worst camera angle is always from below your face, anything from below your face will show all of your chin. You'll be looking down and the camera will be focusing on your chin, and probably on your neck wrinkles.

To get the best angle, look slightly up into the camera. That makes you lift your chin up slightly and it also helps to keep your eyes a little bit more open. To get your computer to your eye level or slightly higher, have your laptop set up on top of a small box or a thick book. You don't want it to be so high up that you can't reach it. Just adjust it until it looks just fine.

3. Avoid Touching Your Phone

Yes, don't touch your phone. Handling your phone when an important webinar is going on won't speak well of you, so keep your phone away unless it necessary. To keep your hands occupied, keep maybe a fine mug in front of you and keep your hand on it if you can't do without touching anything.

4. Put A Little Effort into Your Hair and Makeup

I'm not saying you have to go full-on glam and curl your hair, but where people are going to be basically seeing only your torso, you should try to make that part of you look a little bit better. But you shouldn't make yourself look like someone unrecognizable.

Just put on a little bit of mascara or possibly a neutral lipstick, or maybe just a little lip balm. It can make a big difference.

Also, put in the effort to tidy up and tie your hair or brush it well. Just do whatever you need to do to make yourself look a little bit more presentable. You don't want to go on camera looking dirty.

5. Keep the Distractions To A Minimum And Keep Your Background Neat And Tidy.

This is just basic logic and common sense. Your environment has to be neat and tidy. If you will be doing lots of Zoom video meetings, then it's advisable to permanently setup your study for video meetings.

It always has to be neat so you can sit down any time of day or night. If you get called into a meeting suddenly, you don't want to be scrambling to clean up your filming space. Keep your filming space nice and neat.

Another distraction is when people are staring at themselves in the monitor instead of looking at the people that they're supposed to be talking to you. In a Zoom video meeting, there are like five to twenty little images on the screen and you can see everyone.

It's advisable to look directly at the person you are talking to instead of just staring blanking at the computer. Keep the distractions of playing with your hair, touching your face, pitching your nose, sticking your finger in your ear, to a minimum. No one wants to see that; it can be annoying and gross.

Another distraction that you have to minimize is noise distraction from your family and your pets.

6. Dress Appropriately for Your Business Meetings

Everyone knows that everyone else is working from home, but you definitely shouldn't be wearing an oversized hoodie or something like that. Since you're only filming from the torso up, whatever you're wearing on the top doesn't have to match what you have going on, on the bottom.

You can still have your nighties or your sweats or whatever you want waist down. Just make sure that if you are going to wear your nighties waist down, you have all your things for the meeting assembled in front of you, so that you won't have to get up to get something thereby exposing that you are actually not quite dressed well. It might be embarrassing to you and rude to others in the meeting.

7. Schedule Your Meeting

When you and the colleagues get over a conference depends on the planning you brought into the session. It is not a conference unless you plan. You have to be prepared for your meeting to avoid your time being wasted; thus, pre-plan your meeting. Before the conference starts, here are five items to do:

1. Give Invites in Advance – Meetings should not be a matter of the last minute. The invitations should go at least one day in advance of a structured conference.

2. Distribute the program – A program-less conference is simply a free-for-all. Create a plan and send it to the members so that they can address the subjects.

3. Provide Meeting Materials – When there are advance documents that need to be checked, ensure that they are presented as early as possible so that attendants can correctly interpret them.

4. Schedule Zoom Room – Make sure you arrange an appropriate meeting space that meets the number of participants and the meeting.

5. Set Meeting Goals – Maybe the most crucial thing you should do before the meeting is scheduled is to think about the question, "what is the conference's mission?" The participants want to learn why they are participating in the meeting. This lays forth a reason for the conference. Be concise about the subject of the discussion.

8. Send Invitations to Clients Directly in Calendar Using a Zoom Link

Using Calendar to send direct invitations is an easy way to invite your meeting participants without sending any separate email or text message. You can send direct invitations through the following procedure:

1. Log in to the online server for the Zoom.

2. Tap **Meetings**, in the main section.

3. Click on **Meeting Subject**.

4. There are ways to add to the calendars alongside **Time**.

5. Clicking on **Yahoo Calendar** or **Google Calendar** buttons would immediately create a calendar event in the particular time provided that you pick.

6. Clicking on Outlook Calendar will create an ICS file that will be loaded into your calendar view.

7. You can also copy the details to the conference manually by click on **Copy Invitation**.

8. When you choose **Copy Invitation**, the text of the invitation to attend will open in another tab.

9. Tap **Invitation to Meet** to save.

10. You can copy and submit the invitation via message, or elsewhere.

9. Mute the Microphone When You Are Not Speaking

Ensure your microphone is muted when you are not talking. This minimizes any ambient noise or audio involvement. Use the **Microphone** button at the lower left of the Zoom menu that appears on the conference panel, to silence the microphone. Additionally, you can configure your expectations for Zoom meetings to automatically silence your microphone at the start of each meeting. Using the microphone button to unmute you, hold the enter key for as long as you are speaking. This simple rule provides seamless operation of community meetings or discussions. Use noise cancellation software to elevate the audio quality to the next stage and for more appropriate ambient sound reduction. Muting your microphone can help in listening to lectures attentively and control sounds that can divert your attention.

10.   Inform Participants When You Record Meeting

Until capturing some audio or video conferencing, ensure all members in the meeting:

- Are being watched.

- Are you authorized to record them?

- You may also make this request in writing or report it at the beginning of the conference.

It not only preserves social respect but in certain businesses and regions, consensus rules and regulations could need it.

11.   Ensure Meeting Settings before you Start a Meeting

Owing to technological mishaps, it is highly reasonable for video conferences to be postponed or disrupted. Turn on your computer to ensure it does not happen and test whether Zoom is functioning correctly, at least ten to fifteen minutes before each meeting. Then, if anything goes wrong, alert your meeting organizer as early as possible (if you are the leader, tell your members). Although running a test before each meeting can seem stressful, it is way better than being humiliated or irritated when something terrible happens during your Zoom meeting.

12.   Share Screen when Presenting

Sharing your screen helps meeting participants to understand your topic of presentation. When you are presenting or giving a lecture to your students, make sure you are sharing your screen with them. As an instructor, it will be beneficial for your learners to get an idea of the topic, and they will be able to take part in the discussion. It is not fascinating to attend lectures with voice only. Screen sharing will make speech more interesting, and you can watch any helpful video from YouTube or another website to support your topic.

13.   Create a Meeting Agenda before you Schedule a Meeting

Team members may have difficulty participating efficiently if they do not know whether they should pay attention, give their feedback, or be part of the discussion process. If people assume they are involved in making decisions but you want their feedback only, the end of the discussion is likely to infuriate everyone. Updates are best allocated and perused before the conference, using a small section of the conference to address queries from the participants. If the aim is to make a judgment, state the rule governing the decision. Creating a meeting agenda will help you to pre-plan your meeting so that there will be more opportunities to learn, instead of thinking about what to do next.

CHAPTER 7:

Free Zoom vs Paid Zoom

Free Users

The Zoom application can be introduced in your device or telephone, and you can go to any gathering with a given ID.

Paying Users

In the event that your director framework has a pro, business, or company account, you can download and join Zoom to your device through your work email. At that point, you need to synchronize Zoom with your schedule so you can mastermind Zoom gatherings and welcome far off members to take an interest. Zoom have various highlights for various record type and clients. All clients and record types have highlights custom fitted to their needs.

Sorts of records

There are four (4) sorts of Zoom accounts:

1. Basic or free record

2. Pro record

3. Business or Enterprise account

4. Education record

Zoom empowers one-on-one meetings that can transform into gatherings or group calls, instructional meetings, and online classes for both inside and outside crowds. Zoom allows global video gatherings and meetings with up to 1000 members and participants, and up to 49 recordings on the presentation screen. The free arrangement permits boundless individual gatherings, yet anyway restrains group meetings to 40 minutes and 100 members.

Zoom gives four arrangement types (barring the Zoom Room membership):

Zoom Essential or Free Arrangement

This arrangement is open and fundamental, and permits clients to have a boundless number of individual gatherings and group gatherings with 100 members. It will break after the following 40 minutes if at least three members join the gathering. This record doesn't bolster enormous gatherings, online classes, and meetings. Furthermore, meetings can't be recorded. It additionally empowers a boundless number of eye-to-eye gatherings, video conferencing highlights, web conferencing highlights, and gathering cooperation highlights.

Zoom Pro Arrangement

This arrangement costs $14.99/£11.99 every month per meeting and gathering host, and $12.49 every year. It empowers hosts to make an individual gathering and meeting IDs for Zoom gatherings, and it can record gatherings in the cloud or your device. Be that as it may, it confines the length of gathering gatherings and meetings to 24 hours. It empowers administrators to include orders, 1GB of cloud recording in MP4 or M4A formats, board and use reports, and other discretionary extra highlights.

Zoom Business or Endeavor Plan

This arrangement costs $19.99/£15.99 every month per meeting and gatherings have (10 least). It permits you to customize Zoom gatherings and gatherings with custom URLs and friends marking. It gives records of Zoom gatherings and meetings recorded in the cloud, just as a devoted client service does. It additionally offers at least 10 illustrators, devoted phone support, executive dashboard, records of chronicles in the cloud. The yearly arrangement has even numerous highlights; for example, a customized URL, marked improvement, and customized messages for business and undertakings, and expenses of $16.65 every year.

Zoom Education

Zoom training has boundless distributed storage for chronicles, which is perfect for organizations and associations with more than a thousand representatives. This arrangement costs $19.99/£15.99 every month per meeting and gathering host (100 least) additionally have a customer achievement director.

CHAPTER 8:

Guide For Teachers

Engaging Students in Learning through Zoom Classroom

We all seek to figure out what is the easiest and most practical way to teach each of our courses. If you conclude that you want to pursue synchronous teaching and probably keep office hours with Zoom, below are some helpful ideas for pedagogy.

Manage Participants

If you click at the bottom of the screen on **Manage Participants** (you might have to hover over it), the names of the participants will appear on the right. Participants have the choice to provide input that will help you control the speed of understanding.

Share Screen

Clicking on the **Sharing Screen** icon at the bottom of the screen will give you some choices.

B. Click the **Record** button on the toolbar.

C. Click the **Sharing Screen** button on the toolbar.

D. When the preview screen for the window appears, click on the window you want to share to pick it.

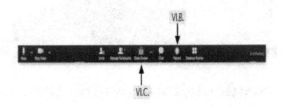

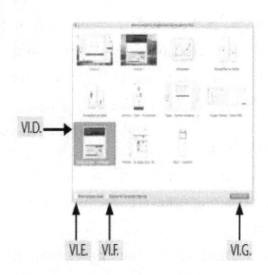

The Whiteboard and the Mac are only two beneficial features.

Desktop: Sharing the computer helps you to queue what you want to reveal ahead of time. You can create an images, music, art, podcasts, and ask students in the chat to respond either verbally respond or annotate on the photo.

Whiteboard

You can consume it on your own or allow students to use it with each other or with you. Mostly it has anonymous participation except for the arrow, which will have the name of the student on it (though not yours). The text size default is 24.

With each quadrant, you can draw a grid asking students to consider another dimension of an item, possibly as a pre-assessment of their awareness of a new topic. Students type their answers into the relevant quadrant. After a simulation of operation, you can use it as a space for reflection.

What were your takeovers of this activity? What ideas would you bring forward? What were your comments?

Check-ins and Breaks

It is called a film strip when the faces of the participants appear linear, and fewer participants will be visible.

Either way, if your course is significant, then not everybody will appear, and at the same time, everybody's face would not be visible to you. Try to click through the faces of the participants as much as possible to try to decide whether they are engaged.

Remember to check in daily. Start the meeting 10 minutes early so students can either speak or use the chat to communicate as they would usually do before class.

Ideas for Using Zoom in Your Synchronous Course

• Bring students together through video/audio conferencing at multiple locations, classroom sites, or field sites.

• Invite guest lecturers for interviews, presentations, and conversations. Record these sessions as instructional material for further use.

• Provide visual meeting space for students abroad and online courses.

• Include virtual office hours of the online courses.

Hosting an Ad Hoc Meeting

1. Start by opening your computer Zoom app.

2. Click on the button **New Meeting**.

3. If you are in the room, click on the **Participants** button at the bottom of the page and then invite more members.

Recording A Meeting With Zoom

• Click on the **Record** button while having a call.

• To access links to the file, go to your browser to *zoom.us./record*. If you are not logged in to your Zoom account, you will be prompted to enter your login credentials.

• Click on the **Distribution** button next to the record you want to spread. Use the connection given to change the sharing settings and distribute them.

Virtual instructions

Live teaching using Zoom

Teachers can schedule Zoom meetings and post the meeting links either from the classroom of their learning management system, or easily in planned and executed documents online.

Students and teachers shall, at the correct time, click on a conference link and execute the class as planned.

Recording live teaching sessions via Zoom

1. Start a meeting with Zoom.

1. Click the **Record** icon .

3. Practice your lesson.

4. End the conference and submit a connection with comprehensive objectives like assignments to the file. (When you want to share the conference, click on the **Require registration** box to see who viewed the video)

Common controls Which Can Be Used In Zoom
Security Icon

Accessible only to Zoom meeting guests and co-hosts, the **Safety** button offers convenient access to a variety of current Zoom protection capabilities as well as a new alternative to turn on an in-meeting Waiting Room. This button helps you to delete participants, lock your group, and determine whether to encourage your respondents to screen share, speak, rename themselves, and post information/annotations.

Managing Members

You can manipulate participants as host of a class/meeting, by renaming, muting, stopping. audio and using other participating member-controls.

ON\OFF Video

When you are in a conference, you can turn on your camera by tapping on the **Play Recording** button at the bottom-left of the page. Click on the **Stop Video** button to turn this off.

Virtual Background

If you are in the conference, you can select a virtual backdrop by click on the **Start Video** icon at the right of the up caret.

Muting

To ensure minimum background noise during a Zoom conference, it is advised that when they are not communicating, you mute everyone on the line. Tap on the **Members** button at the bottom of the screen to do so, and then click on **Mute Everything** in the side window.

Active Learning Strategies for Starting Class

A learning activity can jump-start a class by immediately putting students into the driver's seat of their learning. It's also a powerful way to get a sense of their prior learning so that you can calibrate your instruction to the specific needs of the class. Additionally, active learning, using specific methods, such as **In the News** or the **Sticky Scenario,** can be effective ways to establish the relevance of the subject matter.

#1 Polls

Because the polling tool is built into Zoom, it is relatively easy to set up and employ. Use polls to test comprehension by opening a class with a quick, 3- to 5-question, ungraded quiz. Design these quizzes to assess whether or not students grasp the main concepts in the required reading or other preassigned material. Another approach is to create a short scenario and require students to choose from a multiple-choice list of possible solutions.

#2 Bring Questions

Ask your students to prepare for class by bringing a question that emerged from their reading or perhaps from work on a major paper or project. Invite your students to interject questions when they are most pertinent to the current material. This method is best used throughout the class period but can be a great way to start class. It gets the session underway with an inquiry mindset instead of an information mindset.

Quick Tip: You'll notice Zoom has a **Raise Hand** feature in the **Participants** panel. While a great idea, I find this impossible to monitor. **Reactions**, like the thumbs-up and applause emojis, overlay the video and are more noticeable. However, you have to first define how to use them as there is not yet a **raised-hand** emoji.

However, depending on the age and maturity of your students, that may not be possible. In that case, substituting the **applause**-reaction emoji to symbolize a raised hand is probably the most effective option.

#3 In the News

Prior to class, your students search the news using keywords related to the class topic. Begin the class by asking a few students to screen share an article, provide a summary, and explain its connection to the material.

Alternatively, place students in small groups and have them share their findings. Visit some of the groups so that you are aware of the articles and make reference to them during your instruction.

#4 Define Success

Provide your students with an outline for the class session. Put them in breakout groups, and ask them to discuss what would make the day's class a success for them. Or make this an individual reflection with the instructions, *"Take 2-3 minutes to review the outline and get a sense of what we'll address today.*

Then write out a personal learning goal." Defining the goal helps students to personalize and take ownership of their role in the learning process.

#5 Comprehension Test

Comprehension tests are similar to polling, but are graded. One of my graduate school professors used this method for every class. He began class with a 12- to 15-question quiz on the core concepts of our assigned reading. When complete, we would review the questions and correct answers. During the review, he opened the floor for clarifying questions, and he would lecture only on the material that needed further explanation, ideas we wanted to explore, or theories we didn't yet understand. While Zoom polls can record individual answers, it's a lot of work to get poll results out of Zoom and into your LMS for grading. Instead, I recommend you use the quiz module built into your LMS. These quiz modules have more robust question features, review options, and the grades will go directly into your online grade book.

#6 Prior Knowledge Survey

Prior knowledge surveys differ from polls because they require students to write or type short essay-type responses. The most straightforward method is to give students 2-3 minutes to write out everything they already know about a topic. You can stop there, or ask them to elaborate, going beyond the reading to make connections with their life experience, other classes, documentaries they have watched—anything is fair game. A third phase is to underline or circle what they believe is most relevant, thematic, or important.

After writing, either put students in breakout groups to share what they've circled and underlined or ask a few individuals to share with the entire class.

"The more you can explain about the way your new learning relates to your prior knowledge, the stronger your grasp of the new learning will be, and the more connections you create that will help you remember it later."

—**Peter C. Brown,** Make It Stick: The Science of Successful Learning

#7 What's on Your Mind?

The **What's on Your Mind?** exercise is helpful when the entire class is experiencing something of cultural, personal, or institutional importance that would otherwise distract them. This activity integrates the elephant in the room into the substance of the class session. Start with triad breakout groups and ask students to share what's top-of-mind for them, as they begin class. The question is simple but powerful: "what's on your mind?" Sometimes this is better done in a large group setting, but the drawback is that you only have time for a handful of students to share.

At the time of writing this, we are experiencing the COVID-19 pandemic. An instructor I work with noted that his students were experiencing a high level of anxiety. In response, he started class with a similar exercise and discovered that many of them were worried about completing their internships—a requirement for graduation. While this may have taken away valuable instructional time, it helped to reframe his instruction and to support students in ways that extended beyond the classroom, and further their professional development.

#8 Learning Journals and Journal Reviews

Journals provide students an active outlet while listening to their teacher's instruction, and also a place to record their thoughts. One of the other benefits of journal-during-lecture is that it gives more restless students something to do. One of my friends is a brilliant high school English teacher. He can't sit still in a teacher meeting to save his life, so he doodles. It helps him to listen and pay attention.

The key to making journals like this work is to provide a set of sample prompts.

Note things that most interest you.

Jot down questions—even if they feel unrelated.

Doodle concept maps, create lists, or illustrate ideas.

Just take notes.

If you make this a regular practice in your classroom, you can use journals as a reference point for most other learning activities. An especially effective way to use journals is to begin class by asking students to review their journal entries from the previous class session. Then place students in breakouts to make this a short social learning time. If you want to spend a bit more time here, ask students to make connections between their journal entries and the specific material to be addressed in the current class session. This task will help them connect prior knowledge with the new content.

#9 Sticky Scenario

The **Sticky Scenario** is my favorite activity on this list. The only drawback is that it takes more time and effort to develop. Begin class with a scenario. Embed in the scenario, two to three core concepts you plan to address in your instruction. A scenario differs from a case study in that scenarios are usually imagined and contain less detail. Cases typically draw from real-life circumstances. Like a case, the scenario has to be **sticky**, complicated enough that students cannot default to easy answers. These are often ethical questions and complex problems that require students to stretch into higher-order thinking skills.

In breakout groups, give students several minutes to discuss the scenario, to surface questions, and talk about how they might approach a solution. **The goal here is not to solve the problem as much as it is to understand what's going on.** After small group breakouts, return to the large-group setting. Begin your large-group time by allowing students to ask questions about the scenario. During the teaching segments, use the scenario as an anchor point, referring to it often, allowing it to unfold, and making connections between the scenario and your content.

Quick Tip: You can employ a majority of these methods as either individual or group activities. Group activities take more time. So, if you feel pressured for time, consider retaining a learning activity.

CHAPTER 9:

Create a Virtual Classroom

Symmetric class meetings, through which everybody logs in at a pre-scheduled time to a cloud conferencing program, are one way to create interest and promote collaboration in your complete online courses. Teachers can use a web-conference program in a synchronous session and allow all the students to participate at a pre-scheduled date. The application for video conferencing at the university is Zoom. Zoom may be found on computers, desktops, iPad, smartphones, and even cell devices, enabling students to navigate the class session in several respects.

As a teacher, whether you or your learners have a condition that prevents you from meeting face to face, Zoom will help to keep your class running. Concurrent online class meetings, where everybody is expected to attend a Zoom group, are one way to build interaction while students are far. Still, Zoom may also be used to help special education and learning situations. Zoom may be used on any device and even workstation phones, allowing students to connect with the team meeting in many ways. You can find tips on planning your Zoom meetings in this part, gathering students with the conversation, screen editing, polling, non-verbal reviews and breakdown rooms, and supplying your community with open online learning sessions, as well as resources for different teaching scenarios.

Preparing for Class

Zoom was developed with creativity. Now, if you make confident important choices and familiarize yourself with the application before welcoming students into an informal conference, it works better. Zoom's free edition can provide you with the best performance and features while holding a class. Coach the students to have Zoom activated. Students preparing to attend Zoom meetings from a laptop or computer will also access the application from the Zoom website.

- Get to learn the controls on the server.

- Catch up on managing a quick Zoom meeting.

- Sign up to work out.

- Check the recording and the audio.

- Visit *zoom.us./test* to confirm the internet, video, and audio connections.

- When there are several meeting participants in the same area, only one person can enter the conference with audio to prevent suggestions.

- Find the source of light.

- Make sure a source of light should be in front of you and not behind you.

Schedule Class

Zoom provides webinars and conferences. All formats help you to communicate with students, although some variations do occur. To pick the style that fits better for you, choose the Zoom flowchart or webinar/meeting comparison chart. Go to the Navigation section to the Zoom feature, click on **Plan a New Conference** and obey the directions.

1. Enable your device with the Zoom Windows software.

2. Tap on the upper-left corner button, **Back**.

3. Tap **Schedule**.

4. Enter all related information such as day, year, subject, etc.

5. Select your favorite digital calendar (Google Calendar is perfect if you have got Mail or email accounts), and you will be brought to a page with your Zoom connection.

6. You may give the connection to your students in the meeting scheduler of your online calendar.

When applicable, choose regular meetings such that the URL can stay the same over the course. Try to place a positive name on your conferences. When you intend on learning:

- Meetings of the course occur inside the platform of the Zoom course.

- Recordings can be made accessible automatically via the course page.

- The course meetings can be separated from other conferences.

- Planned meetings often serve as activities for Calendar class participants.

For unplanned events, simply use your meeting ID and official Zoom URL. Such gatherings are not going to have the advantages mentioned earlier, so cannot be hosted by someone else.

Plan Roles

Assigning specific tasks to the students may be an efficient means of coordinating group practice. Often certain students take too much accountability for the activity of a community, while others may be hesitant to commit to the activities of the group. Assigning responsibilities helps to spread liability among group members and guarantees transparency for the involvement of all students. As students practice various roles, they have the chance to develop a wide range of competencies.

The most commonly needed positions for group work include facilitator, planner, and organizer, timekeeper, and issue manager. You would want to create notes of what it feels like when the job is done well and when it is not done well. Ask the students to comment on their perspectives operating in communities in writing or solving issues. Students might still have suggestions for different assigned positions.

When you appoint someone else to handle facets of digital rooms, you will have a less challenging classroom managerial experience. Try requesting one supervisor or student to track the conversation and one to assist their peers with difficulties in technology. Formal identification of alternate hosts may also be created. This way, you will focus on giving lectures and offer some additional technical skills to the students.

Enhance Student's Sense of Community

If everybody reveals their faces through their webcam, the feeling of presence is strengthened. Suggest asking students to click on film as a core component of attendance, because if you can see them, it becomes simpler to communicate with the class, so students are more willing to pay attention because they realize they are on display. Train students about how to turn to the view of the gallery (this is the perspective where everybody is equally accessible to one another).

Suggestions to connect with your students:

- Make eye contact with the camera.

- Mute mics in case you do not participate.

- Find the illumination! Make sure a bright light is in front of you and not behind you.

- Talk in a conversational way; you do not need to talk up.

- Read on to operate a seamless meeting in Zoom for further information.

A good sense of community can boost the class online and lead to student achievement. The culture can be improved if you take action to keep it protected from harassment or disturbance. A few approaches to meet such targets are here:

- Introduce yourself with the safe Zoom meetings setup and guidance.

- Use the regional meeting configuration and in-meeting guidelines to ensure the class is attended only by enrolled learners and invited visitors.

CHAPTER 10:

Common Problems And How To Solve Them

For every video conferencing program, the three most important technological problems are:

- Members could not see.

- Members could not hear.

- External noise and mic problems.

You can overcome technical issues by hosting an online training meeting for reduced stakes, with the primary aim of signing in, troubleshooting technological issues, and getting accustomed to the Zoom application. Get in your meeting early enough to sort out technical problems. Provide a contingency strategy in case of unknown complications or challenges. Students are informed of the backup plan in advance so that if technical issues arise, they can stay on task.

Know how to address these problems by troubleshooting issues. Try informing your community of the *Participant's Guide For Enhancing Your Zoom Performance*. It is recommended to host an online discussion experience with low-stakes introductory meetings, whose primary purpose is to have an entire team login, diagnose problems technical issues, and get used to Zoom functionality.

Create a Teaching Agenda

Prepare for a simultaneous training session online much as you would prepare for an in-person meeting. Discuss the plan with students in advance, and students do have a good understanding of how the curriculum is going to proceed, what is going to be discussed and the events they are going to compete in. Periodically review web behavior and student aspirations or recommend providing a "good management" guide detailing the goals.

Plan for a concurrent session of the course much as you would prepare for knowledge gives the lesson. Here is a testing agenda for a simultaneous sixty-minute instructor meeting to share your agenda with students in advance, so they know what is coming:

- Make students reflect on a problem before joining the digital classroom and write their answers on the whiteboard.

- Using the polling method to ask a question that includes and decides personal significance for the mini-reading subject.

- Linked computers launch PowerPoint and offers mini-readings. To mark the PowerPoint slides, use the annotation functionality in Zoom.

- Render the survey issue provisionally.

- Assign students to separate breakout spaces, chat for ten minutes, and develop a shared Google Report.

- Ask each party to appoint a delegate, to sum up, the main points of their debate.

- Ask students to support the conversation if they are always puzzled.

- Clear up misunderstandings found in the muddiest point of conversation.

- Summarize the session's tasks, set goals for the follow-up events, and achieve them.

Record Your Class

If somebody has a technological problem, you can offer them further access to the course work. You should report the class session to counter this. Record on the web, not on your desktop. Recording in the cloud is easy because you will access both a video URL and an online transcribed clip. Zoom recordings do not have a quota, so records of meetings sessions using Zoom can surface only a few hours.

Begin recording in the appropriate style. Once you start recording, the recording interface is focused on your vision. Note to swap presentations and turn to an active-speaking view rather than a gallery (or do not use the camera), or you will be overlaid in the clip in the upper-right corner. While recording your class, keep in mind certain things:

- Let the students know that you will be recording the class.

- Give students a choice to silence their audio when filming and switching off their camera.

- When meetings are captured in the cloud and you use a module, the recordings can be located right in the PC.

- Such records could be done to specific preservation procedures than other documentation of class sessions.

- For advice about where to place the recordings, and how to show them to your students, contact your local university development help.

- It's no more news that Zoom is one of the foremost online video-conferencing platforms. However, users could encounter a couple of setbacks while using this app. Nevertheless, these glitches can be fixed in no time without requiring a high level of expertise and technical know-how.

The Problem Associated With Audio-Visual

Just in case you joined a meeting and you can't hear anything, there's a likelihood you closed the first screen/window that appeared. Ideally, you should select **Join with computer audio**. Alternatively, tap the spacebar on your computer. If you are using an android device, you can tap the audio button. If the audio is muted, you'll find the microphone sign crossed; you can simply tap this button to unmute it. Also, for your camera/webcam, all you need to activate it is to tap the **Camera** icon, if this doesn't work, you'll have to go to your camera settings and grant access to the app; for a computer, turn on the option of **Allow apps to access your camera** under **Camera Settings**.

In cases with multiple audio-visual devices, make sure the correct device is toggled on in the settings for proper communication. To do this, go to **Settings**, click **Video/Audio** as the case may be, and select the appropriate device.

Problem With Missing Features

There could be an absence of some features when Zoom is being accessed via the web as opposed to via the app. They've also been complaints of longer times being taken for web users to connect to an online meeting. Some don't eventually connect at all. To solve this problem, just download the Zoom app from your Play Store if using an Android device or from your Apple Store if using an iPhone. Then, you can enjoy all the features available to Zoom users.

Problem With Background Noise/Echo

Background noise/echoes are quite common especially when attendees don't mute microphones after joining the meeting, this way different activities occurring in their background creates a nuisance. It's important to note that this problem wouldn't exist if all users muted their microphone with just the mic of the host on, of course.

Notwithstanding, the host can avoid this at the entrance by disabling the microphones of all attendees, hence their microphones are muted by default.

Problem Receiving The Activation Email

At times, it could take a while to receive activation emails, in some cases, just a few seconds, there's no hard and fast rule about it, it will eventually come. You can also check if the email wasn't sent to your spam folder.

The Problem Associated With A Time Limit

Hosts should bear in mind that group meetings are permitted to last for only 40 minutes if you're on the free plan. Once the time elapses, all attendees are disconnected automatically, and the meeting is brought to a sudden end.

Free users can record a meeting on their device, after which they can download the recording to Google Drive or another similar service, and then share it with others. It may or may not be a big deal for you, but it is something to keep in mind.

Problem With Freezing /Lagging During Meetings

A viable way of curtailing this is ensuring that you have good internet access, changing your location could just do the trick. Make sure you also use a reliable internet service provider with a good internet speed {a range of at least 800kbps-1Mbps}

To ensure premium video quality, you should consider disabling the **HD/Touch up my appearance** option; this solves the problem of lagging.

Problem With Zoom Crashing

If the app keeps closing/crashing abruptly, you can check the Zoom service status to rule out the possibility of a locality issue. This can also be experienced when the server is undergoing servicing; it usually returns to normal after servicing is completed.

If it's not a locality issue, you can switch from the app to the web version; this is more efficient in such cases as long as you have good internet access.

It's important to ensure your audio-visuals are routed to the proper channel, audio to speakers, and video to the webcam. Ensure this is done in the settings.

Problem With Zoom-Bombing

Zoom bombing is the deliberate act of disrupting a meeting via the use of various tools like inappropriate videos, gestures, comments. It's become imperative to secure your meetings from ill-meaning individuals.

CHAPTER 11:

Zoom Vs. Other Conferencing Tools

For remote teams, the most preferred collaboration devices are the Zoom, Skype, Facebook rooms, Google Hangouts, Microsoft Teams, ezTalks, Cisco Webex, and BlueJeans, etc.

All of these platforms can be used to hold video calls, chat, and host meetings or webinars. And if you're looking for a new platform to help you do these things, you're probably considering platforms like these.

Ultimately, the variations between all of them may not seem significant. But the decision to implement one over another can still impact your team significantly. It's easy to say from the experiences of a remote team, that every platform fits different needs, and that is why it is important to understand the pros and cons, features, and pricing, etc.

Zoom vs Facebook Rooms

Facebook has finally revealed what its Zoom competitor, Messenger Quarters, can be renamed. The video calling application is integrated into the standalone Facebook Messenger app and is intended for personal use. In comparison, Zoom is based on technical video conferencing. But since both are end-of-day video calling apps, here is a comparison based on functionality, quality of the web, and more.

1) Availability

Both are present in iOS and Android when it comes to availability. It has a web edition that can be obtained from anywhere. This means you can reach it on Windows OS, as well as on macros and ChromeOS. What's more, you don't have to download a separate Messenger Rooms app, as it's built into the Messenger app itself.

2) Free or Not

While Zoom also has a free tier, most of its features are restricted to the paid edition. Zoom has two paid plans costing $14.99 a month, and $19.99 a month. However, up to 100 participants are still in favor of the free version.

3) Characteristics

In this one, Zoom gets an edge, as the video conferencing application can support up to 100 participants in one call session. The paid version can support 350-500 participants. At the moment, Facebook Messenger rooms are limited to 50 participants.

Yet, when it comes to video call size, Messenger is taking the lead. It allows you to speak with 50 people for unlimited minutes at a time, whereas Zoom's free tier can support 100 (or less) participants in a 40-minute call. The paid version can support calls up to 24 hours.

Since Zoom is designed for organizational use, it also has the function of call recording, and something is missing from Messenger Room right now. The biggest advantage of Facebook is the audience that it already has in the main app and the Messenger app. Using news feed, groups, and events, you can start and share rooms on Facebook, and it's comfortable for people to drop by.

Facebook says it will quickly add ways to create Instagram Direct, WhatsApp, and Portal rooms. Both Facebook and Zoom offer the versatility to communicate via text during a video call and share screens with others.

Skype vs Zoom

Several applications for video conferencing are on the market. Skype is among the competition's largest and oldest brands. It allows single-to-one video calls, instant messaging, screen sharing, group calls, and file sharing, much like Zoom.

Skype redirects messages to an email inbox for those who participate offline. Skype is still lagging behind its competition, though, in that the platform only allows up to ten participants at a time. A no-go definitely to larger conferences.

According to Global Industry Forecasts, video conferencing is expected to become a 20-million-dollar industry by the end of 2024.

Below is a comparison of Zoom's and Skype's features, pricing, and product performance to best serve video conferencing needs.

Zoom

It's an innovative cloud-based with modern conference tools. Zoom derives breakout sessions that can be used to divide your viewers (e.g., customers or employees) into small groups like webinar training, specific topics, or some online class discussions.

The organizer has the power to monitor the meeting with Zoom. You can also mute all microphones when not in use, monitor presentation access for the attendants, and so on. Besides, this method allows the participants to participate by digitally raising their hands to the discussion.

The chat utility of Zoom also allows viewers to communicate directly with your instructor and with other participants, thus ensuring a collective classroom setup.

General Information

When considering Skype vs Zoom, the biggest challenge is that they are both very powerful channels of communication. Deciding between these two can be difficult, as both are efficient and cost-effective. By definition, Zoom is a software-based on video or audio conferencing that was intended to promote collaboration through an advanced integrated system featuring web conferences, group messaging, and important online meetings. On the opposite hand, Skype provides powerful tools for text, voice, and video, providing users with a smart way to share their experiences with others, no matter where they are.

Devices

Zoom supports web platforms such as Android, iPhone, Mac, and iPad.

The web-based Skype supports all Windows and Android devices, and iPhones. Zoom has a variety of features, including video conferences, streamlined scheduling, and collaboration between groups. This platform's other powerful features include local and cloud recording in premium audio feature, and in Zoom Meetings and Zoom Rooms. Skype also comes with powerful chat tools, including Skype-to-Skype calls, community calls, call-forwards, one-to-one video calls, and instant messaging. You can send and exchange emails, video messages, displays, files, and contacts.

Clients

Zoom and Skype both deliver premium video conferencing solutions — a factor that contributes to their loyal customers around the globe.

Designed for

Both Zoom and Skype are perfect for small businesses and large business, but freelancers are also popular with Skype's free plan.

Pricing

Zoom offers four pricing packages for enterprises: Zoom Basic Plan, Zoom Pro Plan, Zoom Business Plan, and Zoom Enterprise Plan.

Basic Plan

The basic package — which is explicitly tailored for personal meetings — is free, can host up to 100 people, and provides one-on-one sessions without restrictions.

It's an excellent gratuitous bid.

You can use this program to:

- Have team meetings of up to forty minutes

- Have a plethora of meetings

- Get online support

- Enjoy the functions of web and video conferencing

- Make sure community collaboration is safe

Zoom Pro Plan

It is for the small teams, and it costs $14.99 per user per month.

This program also includes business inter-operability user management tools, admin controls, REST API, and Skype. Users can store and share large amounts of data with 1GB data of MP4 and M4A cloud recording. The optional Zoom add-on plans

This include five sub-plans:

$40 a month for extra cloud recording storage

$49 per month for 323/ SIP Room Connector

$49 a month for joining Zoom Rooms.

$100 a month for toll-free dialing/Call Me.

$40 a month for adding video webinars.

Business Plan

The business strategy for the Zoom, which is worth $19.99 a month per user, is limited to smaller businesses. Equipped with all of the Pro plan's functionality, mid-sized companies will use it to take their connectivity to another level.

The plan lets you host up to 10 hosts. It has admin control dashboard, telephone support, and a vanity URL. A business plan is an excellent option if you prefer on-premise placement. Certain characteristics of the scheme are:

- Manage domains and one-way sign-on

- Client branding and customized emails

- Integration with LTI

Zoom Plan for Enterprise

Zoom Enterprise is for $19.99 per person/host per month. This plan, which includes all of the Business Plan features, needs you to have a minimum of 100 hosts. Up to 200 participants are allowed into this plan.

The Enterprise package is ideal for large organizations with diverse meeting needs, and offers unrestricted cloud storage, a zealous client service manager, and executive company feedback.

Skype

Imagine communicating with your employees directly from your PC/phone through an instant short messaging service, screen sharing, file sharing, and informal/formal audio or video calls. Effective and direct—that is what Skype is all about.

Skype is designed to make simple communication using revolutionary technology. Its intuitive chat interface, like Zoom, allows users to send prompt messages to other users. Users can integrate video with audio from their chat windows without any effort.

Skype is free of charge. However, if you're looking to improve efficiency and increase revenue, Skype has a $2-per-month enterprise price package per user.

Business Plan
Online Plan 2

This plan costs $5.50 a month per user and is designed for online business meetings. You can use Online Plan 2 to:

Join any meeting

Enjoy HD video in the group as well as audio-calling (for 250 people)

Receive mobile technical assistance at the client level

Office versions available online

50 GB Postbox

1 TB Store File

Office 365 Professional Premium

This plan is for $12.50 per user per month. The Office 365 Company Critical plan has notable features, including:

Government software pre-installed on PC/Mac

Tablet and mobile apps

In addition, Skype's parent company, Microsoft, has supported Microsoft Teams over Skype as a forum for meeting and video conferencing. As a result, Skype support may diminish in favor of Teams over time.

Backend Integrations Zoom

Zoom supports

Microsoft One Drive

Salesforce Box

Slack

Okta

Microsoft Outlook

LTI (Canvas, Desire2Learn, Backboard, and Moodle)

Google Chrome

Marketo

Facebook Centrify

Intel Unite

Kubi

Zapier

RSA

Other integrations that Zoom supports include:

Google Drive, DropBox, Pardot

Firefox and Acuity Calendar

Eloqua and the Microsoft Active Directory

Hipchat, Infusionsoft, and HubSpot

Provides integration with programs such as:

Office (Word, Lync, Outlook, PowerPoint)

WordClick on

Mendix

Lucid Meetings

OnePage CRM

Bitium

Cayzu Helpdesk

BigContacts

SalesExec

Interactive Intelligence CaaaS

1CRM

Grasshopper

Slack

GroupWise

Skype can also be integrated with other systems, such as:

CRM Agile

Wimi and 88 Center for Virtual Touch

Microsoft Dynamics Online CRM

The Concierge and Yugma Moxie

Zoom vs Skype: The Low Line

Zoom and Skype both deliver customized solutions and are designed to take interactions from your company to the next level. But the free and paid third-party apps enhance Zoom and give it a slight edge.

CHAPTER 12:

Zoom vs Google Hangouts

In 2013, Google Hangouts was released as a way to merge previously separate apps from the company, Google Talk (for calls), Google+ Messenger (for chat), and the original Google+ Hangout (for video), into one. Over time, the platform has added voice calling and video calling to accommodate all types of virtual conversation.

Zoom was released the same year, but in 2017, according to The Business Journals, it started climbing up ranks of app charts. It has since gained traction — especially during the recent outbreak, when many people turn to the app for their (professional or personal) video conferencing needs, according to CNBC. Although both channels are useful at the core for staying linked during these social distancing and self-quarantining times, some main features make them unique.

1) **Number of Participants**

The number of people a video conference app allows you to have in one meeting could be a make-or-break point for you, depending on whether you want to have huge company-wide meetings (or you are just super-popular).

By contrast, Zoom allows users to have a video call with up to 100 participants. The Gallery View feature lets you see up to 49 of those participants on one screen. Plus, if you want an even bigger meeting, you can have up to 500 people (as long as you get the $50-month Large Meeting add-on).

2) Price

If you're only searching for a video-conferencing device for friends and personal use, you may want to invest as close to nothing as you can.

If you only want to use Google Hangouts to make and receive phone and video calls, you can do this at no charge. But, if you wish for storage to keep records of your meetings and calls, pricing for 30 GB of storage starts at $6 per month.

Zoom has various packages, priced depending on how many features are included. The free choice allows you to have unlimited meetings with up to 100 people. You pay $14.99 a month for a Pro account (meaning for small teams) per host.

3) Additional Characteristics

Not everybody is using video-conferencing software for video calls only. Often, it's good to learn that your apps can do more.

If you're searching for something a little easier, then your best bet is Google Hangouts. The software does have additional features, but most do not require extra practice. These include group conferencing, intelligent changeover, and integration with other Google apps. Most of the time, you can only log into and start using Google Hangouts.

At first, Zoom may seem a little more complicated, but it provides a great set of additional features if you'd like some fun. They provide a note-taking annotation tool, an automated transcript-creator, and even a touch-up feature.

4) <u>Capabilities of Screen Sharing</u>

Whether you're in a coworker meeting or talking to friends about that strange thing your cat did when no one was looking, you sometimes need visual aids. If you're already on a video call, this is where the applications for screen sharing come in. Google Hangouts allows you to share your computer in the video call with others, but it is bounded to one user at a time.

By contrast, Zoom allows multiple people to share their screens at once within meetings.

5) <u>GIFs & Emojis</u>

This may not be the most prominent feature you're looking for, but sometimes your messages just need a little more fun. While this feature is more for those who talk with friends, you never know when you want to give a cool "thumbs-up" emoji to your boss.

Although Zoom does not let you use emojis, it does allow you to use GIFs. Plus, it will allow admins to turn on and off the feature. This could be useful during meetings which are all-business. But even so, you can still use the whiteboard capabilities of Zoom to draw on various slides and screens, so there is a way to get around that.

6) Time Limit

When you are searching for a video conferencing device for work meetings, the time limit for video chatting may not matter as much.

Google Hangouts has no known limitations regarding the length of calls you can make to others. Nevertheless, Zoom has a limit for those using its free package. Though you can make infinite numbers of calls, each call will last only up to 40 minutes. If you use a Pro account, or anything more expensive than that, the limit will move up to 24 hours.

Aside from learning about the features of an app, often it just takes you to use it and compare it to others firsthand to find out which choice is better for you. Happy chatting anyway!

CHAPTER 13:

How to Deal with Zoom Bombing

A s it's often the case in medicine, there are no surgeries without complications. Similiarly, regardless of the pros of the Zoom platform, if adequate measures aren't put in place to secure the platform during meetings, training, seminars, there could be an invasion by miscreants.

Zoom bombing is an intentional attempt to interrupt a meeting by an individual or a group of people, commonly known as trolls.

A few tips to help secure your meetings include:

Ensure your meeting has a password.

Enable waiting rooms to curtail the influx of attendees.

Prohibit unnecessary screen-sharing.

Disable the **Join Before Host** option so the meeting doesn't commence without you.

Lock the meeting.

Ensure Your Meeting Has A Password

The most rudimentary way of ensuring security in your Zoom meeting is to create a password for meetings; it restricts intrusion by gatecrashers.

Sometime in April 2020, Zoom modified their basic and pro accounts making it a sine qua non that meetings must have a password by default, including previously scheduled meetings.

Make sure your meetings have a password.

Log into your Zoom portal, click on **My Account**, then select **Settings** and then click **Meeting**.

Require a password when scheduling new meetings.

Require a password for instant meetings.

Require a password for participants joining by phone.

These measures ensure that all new invites are expected to input the password. Meetings can be scheduled using a personal meeting ID as well as a general meeting ID. Additional security settings are also encouraged. An option includes disconnecting your meeting password from the URL link; this ensures the attendee who has the link still has to manually input the password. To do that click **My Account**, then **Settings** > **Meeting.** Select **Embed Password in meeting link for one-click join** and disable it.

Avoid Broadcasting Your Meeting Publicly

Putting up your meeting details on certain social media handles increases the risk of a breach in privacy as it could fall into the wrong hands, Zoom makes provision for messages to be sequentially sent to both panelists and attendees before and after the event, which are secure. Attendees should be intimated on the importance of securing their meeting URL.

Once your meeting password has been enabled, attendees who have been approved will receive the link and password via their invites.

Enable Waiting Room To Curtail The Influx Of Attendees

This feature gives you the privilege to scrutinize every one that participates in your meeting. You're fully aware of those that have joined the meeting as well as the absentees. It serves as a form of surveillance. To activate this feature, select **My Account**, select **Settings,** and then tap the **Meeting** bar. You'll find the waiting room bar as you scroll down; click on it. Two options will pop up: **All participants** and **Guest participants**. The former places everyone in the waiting room awaiting the host's approval, while the latter keeps unrecognized participants in the waiting room for scrutiny {this is less stressful}.

On the other hand, the Waiting Room tab can be disabled while the meeting is on-going. To do this, click on the **Security** tab, turn off the **Enable waiting room** option, you can now manually add attendees to your meeting. To do this, click on **Participants**. If you wish to add attendees one after another, click admit just by the names of the participants, on the contrary, if you know all the attendees in the waiting room, you can add them all by clicking **Admit All**

The Zoom app is designed in such a way that participants can share the contents of their device screen. However, the host can put some restraining limits on what can be shared. This can be achieved by putting up some security measures.

The Zoom portal has a **Security** button. By clicking on it, you'll find the bar Allow Participants to. This allows them be able to share their screen or change their name. Disabling this limits the attendees' ability to screen share or change names.

The host reserves the right to decide to be the only one with the privilege to share their screen.

With the meeting going on, tap the arrow to the right of the Screen Share tab, and select **Advanced Sharing Options**; click who can share and choose **The Host Only** option

Disable Join Before Host So The Meeting Doesn't Start Without You

To ensure orderliness is maintained in a Zoom online meeting, it's advised that the host arrives at the meeting before the attendees, you can beef up security by disabling the **Join Before Host** setting. To do this, go to **My Account** in your Zoom portal. Click on **Settings**, then **Meeting**. Keep scrolling till you see the **Join before host** tab; turn it off.

Lock The Meetings

Locking meetings once they begin is also another option that should be considered. Information can be passed to attendees about the time allowed for them to join the meeting before the meeting is locked. The host reserves the right to do this. To enable this, go to the **Security** button, turn on the **Lock meeting** option.

CHAPTER 14:

How to Record Zoom Meetings

It can be difficult to remember every point discussed during a meeting, especially if you covered more than one topic. Instead of taking notes, you can record Zoom meetings and watch them when you need important information.

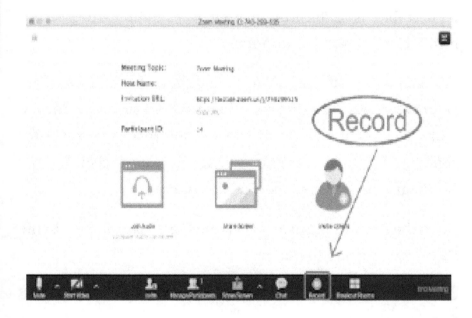

Additionally, recording a Zoom meeting will allow you to share the discussed details with your colleagues who were unable to attend the meeting.

How to Record A Zoom Meeting From A PC Or Mac

When you need a meeting recording, Zoom has two ways to choose. Both the free and paid versions of Zoom provide a local recording feature that allows users to store recorded clips on their local hard drives. Free local registration is provided. While corresponding cloud registration is available at a starting price of $14.99/month for pro-size hosts, it works well for small teams. With a midsize business starting with 10 hosts, this offer is $19.99/month for business. Finally, the highest bid is Enterprise for $19.99/month for100-people host for the largest organization.

You should specify the folder where your file will be saved before starting a meeting recording to avoid searching for the folder that is automatically created for this purpose. After running the Zoom Desktop Client, you must click on the **Settings** icon to access the settings window.

Go to the Recording tab and click the **Open** button next to the **Save recordings to** option.

Click the toggle button **Next** to the local log option, if the feature is not activated.

Zoom also allows you to enable this feature on all groups you create with it. Click on the **Group Management** icon, find the group for which you want to enable this option and go to the Settings tab. Open the Registration tab and enable the local registration option if it is disabled.

How To Record Local Zoom Meetings

Start the Zoom meeting when you're ready and tap the record button. If a menu appears on your screen, you must choose the recording option on this computer and a small recording tape will be displayed in the lower right corner of your screen.

After pausing the recording, Zoom will convert the meeting recording so that the file is accessible. Once the conversion is complete, the destination folder will appear on the screen so you can quickly preview the video.

Locate the Menu bar and select the **Record** button.

Can't locate your recorded file? Open the program; find and click the meeting. Select the recorded option. Once opened you will find the recorded files. Managing recorded files is simple. You can choose to open the file, play the recorded video directly, or play only the audio.

Record A Rounding Meeting With 3ʳᵈ Party Software

One of the options is to use *Filmora scrn* to record a Zoom meeting, especially when you cannot record Zoom meetings with the built-in Zoom tool.

Whether in a small meeting or on a larger scale, this option provides another way to take advantage of Windows and Mac systems.

First of all, download and install *Filmora scrn*.

Once the program starts, you will need to choose **Start** to start recording if you want to get the full settings.

You have four options in this area: screen, audio, camera, and fireplace. If you need to use the sound, choose the option you choose by clicking on the icon. Finish the step by clicking **Settings** to make any adjustments before recording begins.

At this point, select the video of the meeting with Zoom and start recording by clicking **Capture**. You will get a countdown from 3 to 1. Immediately after the count is complete, click on **F10** to stop recording. Alternatively, customize a quick on/off switch in the Setup menu. When complete, the file will be placed in the library where you can select it for further editing or share it if perfect.

How To Record A Zoom Meeting From iPhone Or Android

It is not possible to record meetings locally from iPhone and Android devices. You must purchase one of the available subscription plans to access Zoom's cloud registration feature.

With the cloud registration option, you can share, view, or download records directly from your Zoom account.

Click on the **More** icon as soon as you start a meeting from your iPhone and choose the cloud recording option from the menu.

The recording bar will appear in the upper-right corner of your screen to inform you that the recording session is in progress. You can pause the recording by clicking on the **More** icon; your videos will be placed in a **My Recordings** folder that can be accessed from a web browser.

The process of recording a Zoom meeting from an Android phone is similar to the one just described. Once the Zoom meeting starts, you need to click on the **More** icon and choose the recording option.

How To Record Zoom Meeting In The Cloud

However, cloud storage is limited to 1GB or 0.5GB for most subscription plans only. You need to make an additional purchase if you want more storage space.

The cloud registration option may be disabled by default, so if you want to enable it in your account, in a group you have created for end-users, you must follow the steps below.

Log in to your account as an administrator who has permission to change account settings. Click the **Account Management** option in the Navigation pane. Go to **Account Settings**, open the Registration tab, and activate cloud registration. Optionally, you can disable the cloud log download option if you don't want anyone to download your videos.

If you want to enable cloud registration for a group you created, you must click the **User Management** menu and then select the **Group Management** option. Find the group for which you want to enable this option; click on it, and then click on the **Settings** button. Go to the Recording tab and activate the cloud recording function.

End-users can activate cloud registration by clicking the **Settings** button in the Navigation pane and opening the Registration tab. After that, you just have to activate the cloud registration option and confirm the changes you made.

Zoom allows you to customize cloud recording settings once the option is enabled so you can choose the recording layout, or if you want to record audio-only or save chat messages from the meeting. Additionally, you can automatically transcribe audio recordings, add timestamps to video recordings, or choose to display the names of the recording participants.

When you're ready, you should start a new meeting, but be aware that only hosts and hosts can start a new cloud sign-in session. Click the **Register** button and choose the cloud registration option from the drop-down menu.

How To Record Texts

In addition to recording Zoom meetings, you can also automatically copy the meeting sound that you record in the cloud. As the host of the meeting, you can edit the text, scan the text for keywords to access the video now, and share the recording.

Conclusion

Since this global pandemic, several in-office teams have failed to connect efficiently. Using the right video conference method like Zoom will also help you cross most of the gaps well. You are all ready to host your video calls to plan initiatives, evaluate team results, and participate in interactive team-building events. When you operate a remote staff, Zoom can help you keep in contact with them through its amazing features of video conferencing. While text message and email can also boost the connection, you are likely to improve work engagement and task performance when you see your coworkers.

Zoom can suit any workflow and can be used on a laptop or smartphone device. Such versatility is ideal for remote workers as any worker will function in a way that fits them better from wherever they may be. Better possible, by utilizing Zoom on your devices instead of your computers, you would not have to compromise functionality or vice versa. The features that list in this book can be used on all platforms, digital environments, screen sharing, etc. Zoom has eased your search if you are searching for a lightweight approach for video calling.

Not only is Zoom ideal for one-on-one meetings, but also community events of 100+ participants can often be held with the Zoom. The built-in collaborative effort tools such as co-annotations, personal as well as community chat groups, shared calendars, and polling features can also be used. To put it another way, team meetings held with Zoom sound like in-person sessions. Zoom is the unchallenged pioneer in the field when it comes to video chat applications. Its mixture of in-depth functionalities, user design, and flexible pricing structure makes it a worthwhile addition to the software platform of any business. Just note to take maximum advantage of all tools that are described in this book. If you do, you will feel all the benefits that Zoom gives.

CPSIA information can be obtained
at www.ICGtesting.com
Printed in the USA
BVHW041025031220
594764BV00006B/87